REPORTING THE KENNEDY ASSASSINATION

REPORTING THE KENNEDY ASSASSINATION

Journalists Who Were There Recall Their Experiences

Proceedings of "Reporters Remember: 11/22/63"
A Conference Held November 20, 1993, at Southern Methodist University

LAURA HLAVACH AND DARWIN PAYNE, EDITORS

THREE FORKS PRESS
P.O. BOX 823461
DALLAS, TEXAS 75382

LIBRARY OF CONGRESS CATALOG CARD NO. 96-061385

ISBN: 0-9637629-2-3

PRINTED IN THE UNITED STATES OF AMERICA

FOREWORD

Here are the memories of a large number of journalists who were either in Dallas or arrived there immediately after the assassination of President John F. Kennedy on November 22, 1963. Their recollections of that fateful weekend, Friday through Sunday, are far more than just fascinating. They add important new information about how the journalists responded to the challenge of this sudden and tragic event and also what they witnessed as first-hand observers, beginning with President Kennedy's arrival in Dallas and ending with the shooting on November 24 of Lee Harvey Oswald by Jack Ruby.

The occasion for these recollections was a reunion called "Reporters Remember: 11/22/63," held on the campus of Southern Methodist University in Dallas to commemorate the thirtieth anniversary of the event. A local committee of reporters sought to identify all journalists (print, broadcast, photographers, cameramen) who were in Dallas that weekend and to extend to them an invitation to attend the meeting. Almost all of those who attended were Dallas or Fort Worth journalists.

Much attention has been focused on the actions of high-profile journalists who either came to Dallas as quickly as possible after the assassination or were a part of the press corps accompanying President Kennedy. However, as these recollections will demonstrate, local news media, whose numbers were far greater and who had the advantage of knowing intimately the city and its law enforcement officers, were much closer to all aspects of the story. Their insights are surprisingly enlightening for anyone who seeks to understand the events of that weekend from almost any point of view.

The transcripts that follow were taken from videotapes of the conference. Every attempt has been made to accurately reflect what was said.

CONTENTS

OPENING COMMENTS

REMARKS BY DARWIN PAYNE, CONFERENCE COORDINATOR

After registration and coffee from 8 to 8:30 a.m., the day-long session convened at 8:30 a.m., Saturday, November 20, 1993, in the Ballroom of the Umphrey Lee Center on the campus of Southern Methodist University in Dallas, Texas. The journalists sat together at the front of the auditorium. Behind them were spectators who had paid $10 each for admission. A large number of news media representatives were present to cover the event.

Good morning. Welcome to Reporters Remember: 11/22/63. On behalf of Southern Methodist University, I

Payne

extend to you a very cordial greeting and a sincere thanks. Thanks especially to all you journalists who covered the Kennedy assassination thirty years ago and who agreed to return for this event at your own expense. It's great to be together again; there can be no question about that. And thanks also to all of you interested citizens who have come to hear us relive our memories—individuals who have come, I might add, from as far away as Finland. Thanks also to the news media who are here reporting on our proceedings today and relaying them to a far greater audience.

I'm Darwin Payne, head of the journalism sequence, Center for Communication Arts, Southern Methodist University. Thirty years ago I was a reporter for the *Dallas Times Herald.*

This promises to be a very exciting day. And—there can be little doubt—an important day. Our recollections are being permanently recorded for future historians, students, and other interested persons by my colleagues in SMU's television-radio program. The entire videotape record will be maintained here as primary source material for those who in the future may study that weekend and the media's involvement. We intend also to create a one-hour summary tape and to make it available for wider dissemination.

Gathered in this room are some sixty journalists—reporters, editors, photographers, and TV cameramen—who were here in Dallas that fateful weekend covering the visit of President John F. Kennedy. We will hear from them vivid recollections of the fast-moving events of that weekend. A dozen or so who are here actually heard the shots at Dealey Plaza; two of you were in the Texas Theater when Lee Harvey Oswald was captured; several were in the police basement when Jack Ruby shot Oswald. Some who are here even served as pallbearers for Oswald—there was no one else there to perform that task.

We can take a look at ourselves and see that we represented thirty years ago a different era in journalism and in American society. We were the last of a particular generation, a generation that now seems greatly outdated. We were almost all men—white men, at that. The few women in the business were inevitably assigned to the women's pages. And there were practically no minorities in any of the media.

Far more than usual, I would say, the news media was prepared to cover every aspect of President Kennedy's visit to Dallas. The reason for this was that, frankly, we anticipated, we feared trouble. Only a month earlier in Dallas UN Ambassador Adlai Stevenson had been banged over the head with a demonstrator's sign and spat upon as he was surrounded by a an angry mob of right-wing demonstrators. In light of this, some had urged that the president cancel his trip to Dallas for fears of his safety.

Arriving in Dallas with President Kennedy were nearly sixty reporters and photographers who were a regular part of the president's press corps. They had been joined on the Texas tour by a handful of Texan journalists. All or practically all of these newsmen were riding in the two press buses and a photographer's convertible in the motorcade.

In Dallas awaiting the president and stationed at various points were local reporters and editors and photographers and cameramen. They were from the *Dallas Morning News,* the *Dallas Times Herald,* the local TV stations, and a handful of radio stations that aggressively covered the news. Soon arriving after the shots were fired were journalists from the *Fort Worth Star-Telegram* and the *Fort Worth Press.* Scores of other journalists flew here from across the country that Friday afternoon, and also from throughout the world. It has been estimated that as many as 300 persons were here on that weekend on the various news teams.

The manner in which we journalists covered the most momentous single event of the century already has been widely discussed and scrutinized. Some have praised the press for rapidly disseminating to an anxious, traumatized nation the news of the assassination and the immediate developments afterwards. Television viewing reached the highest level in its history; many have said TV news came of age during those four days. Some have criticized the press for its performance; some have even tied it into a conspiracy.

Here today we have gathered in one place the largest number of journalists who covered the assassination. What follows is not an assessment of our performance, although there likely will be some of that. What we are about to do primarily will be to describe the events that we saw unfold before our own eyes and to describe how we covered the story.

While it surely is true that no single journalists had a clear, definitive view of the swirl of events occurring that weekend, it is equally true that in a group such as this certainly a clearer picture may emerge. And that's the spirit of our meeting today, an opportunity to hear one another and to compare notes and perhaps even to correct or adjust our memories.

Now, on to some basic information. As you will see on your program we have organized a number of panels to kick off our discussions of the various events and sites of that weekend thirty years ago. After our panelists we will go to our participating journalists, many of whom will have vivid memories of their own on the subject or who may have pertinent questions. A microphone has been placed on the floor just for you.

Members of the audience are encouraged to write down their questions and to give them to our student monitors, who will give the questions to the moderators.

We're also going to conduct a poll today. You will have been handed a half-sheet of paper with a few questions that will ask you your opinions about the assassination. There is one poll for our audience and another for our journalists. We'll tabulate these and announce the results at the end of the day.

Now, we have a busy, intriguing day before us. Let's get started.

INSTANT DECISIONS: DIRECTING THE COVERAGE

EDDIE BARKER, Moderator

The shots fired at Dealey Plaza shattered elaborate plans carefully made by the news media, especially the local media, for covering the presidential visit. New and critical judgments—entirely different from original ones—had to be made. Reporters, photographers, and cameramen had to be directed to new locations now deemed critical such as Dealey Plaza, Parkland Hospital, and the Dallas police station. (This session began at 8:35 a.m. and ended at 9:30 a.m.)

Introduction of Barker by Darwin Payne: Some of the most important decisions or perhaps the most important decisions were made behind the scenes in the newsrooms. Decisions such as when to release information, how late to hold up deadlines, where to send photographers, reporters and many other things. The moderator for this panel, Eddie Barker, was the news director for both TV and radio as well as the on-air anchor for KRLD Channel 4 in Dallas, a multiple role that today is unheard of in such a large market.

As Eddie himself puts it, little is known about his early years, although he admits to being born in San Antonio. He made it through high school, got himself hired as the youngest announcer ever on the old Humble Southwest Conference football circuit.[1] And when Channel 4 went on the air in Dallas on December 3, 1949, he was there. He stayed there until 1972 when he left the news business. Eddie broke some sensational stories over the years, among them the Franklin Speers story in which the doctor blew up an airplane after having a friend take his seat on it. He also had the first television interview with Marina Oswald.

Eddie's was almost assuredly the most familiar face in Dallas as he delivered the news every night on KRLD-TV. That familiarity perhaps is what led a Parkland doctor to confide to Eddie early on that Friday afternoon that the president was dead. Eddie, feeling confident of his source's knowledge, announced the president's death over KRLD and CBS without official confirmation. He stuck to his guns, despite network fears that it was premature. *Journalism Quarterly*, the scholarly publication for the profession, called his decision one of the greatest snap evaluations of a source in the history of broadcast journalism.[2] At this year's RTNDA[3] meeting, the members named a special award for Eddie to commemorate forever his achievement.

---

[1] Humble Oil & Refinery, now Exxon Corp., for many years sponsored Saturday afternoon play-by-play radio broadcasts of Southwest Conference college football games that gained wide audiences.

[2] The incident occurred at the Trade Mart, where Barker was among the many who were stationed there awaiting the president's arrival. A physician who was on the staff at Parkland Hospital approached Barker and told him that he had learned from the hospital's Emergency Room that the president was dead. Barker, who recognized the physician but did not know his name, was convinced that the information was accurate. He instantly decided to broadcast the fact of the president's death. "When I announced this over the air," Barker later said in an interview, "the network panicked. No official announcement had yet been made, and the validity of my source was questioned. However, I knew that this man was trustworthy; so, I kept repeating that the president was dead." The author of the article in *Journalism Quarterly* wrote that "in the absence of official confirmation, [this] may be the most important journalistic event of the period; it will certainly be one of the greatest snap evaluations of a source in the history of broadcast journalism." Richard K. Van der Karr, "How Dallas TV Stations Covered Kennedy Shooting," *Journalism Quarterly* 42 (1965), 646-47.

[3] Radio-Television News Directors Association.

These days Eddie is involved with the meeting, planning and convention business through his public relations firm, Eddie Barker and Associates. He's married, has five children, including a daughter who is a reporter and a son who is a secret service agent. And he has nine grandchildren. Eddie Barker.

Barker: Thank you very much, Darwin. And, as you said, we call our first panel here "Instant Decisions: Directing the Coverage," and very frankly I can't think of a time in history when it was more important to make a decision very quickly and then hope to God that you were right.

Barker

This panel that we have with us this morning are the folks that had to make some of those decisions, and I think that history has pretty well recorded that the decisions they made at the time were decisions that they can still live with 30 years later.

I was in the decision-making business then, too. One of the things that I think that we really have to think about as we reminisce of what happened back then was the tools that we had to work with thirty years ago compared to the tools that we have to work with today. In television, of course, we had black and white film. We had old DH and DL cameras that we hope we had the good sense to pull the filter out of when we went inside to take inside footage. We knew how to run an Auricon camera, make a tape recording. Hopefully we knew how to edit film, how to write to film, and how to go on the air.

With this visit of the president coming to Dallas, my newsroom as all newsrooms decided that we really had to do this one first-class. And the reason, not only because it was the visit of a president, but because as Darwin mentioned a minute ago there were so many things going on in Dallas and in the Texas Democratic Party that it was going to be a fun day for sure. One of the things that you may not remember is the fact that the Democratic Party was pretty much split down the middle in those days, and then Senator Ralph Yarborough refused to ride in same car with Vice President Lyndon Johnson in that parade;[4] that was the bitterness of this thing. It was the reason that the president came to Dallas in the first place—to try to heal some of these wounds, not only here in Dallas but all over the state.

So we turned out our entire newsroom that day. For television, for radio, and for four hours of talk radio we had a total 31 people. By today's standards, I don't think that was very many. We covered the event. Certainly those were a couple of our guys on the tape that you heard there; I recognize Bob Huffaker is with us today, and Wes Wise, filmed the shot, a lot of it by George Phenix, who is also here with us today, and you will be hearing from all of them later.

As far as another reason for our trying to plan excellent coverage was the fact that the Adlai Stevenson incident that Darwin referred to. Wes Wise, who then was our sportscaster as well as a newscaster as well as a cameraman and everything else and later mayor of Dallas—I won't tell you how he got to be mayor of Dallas because it is a little embarrassing, but back in those days we had—we started talk radio in this market, and we had a show called "Comment," and it ended every afternoon with what we called "the great garage sale of the air," and Wes Wise sold more baby buggies and mattresses, etc., than anybody in memory and it got him into the mayor's office in Dallas. Those were different times too because reporters trusted cops, cops trusted reporters, and as these panels go on today, you are going to wonder if the Dallas Police Department wasn't the private taxi service of such notables as Hugh Aynesworth and Jim Ewell.

Well, so much for my rambling. Let's get to some of these guys who had to make some of those very tough decisions. And one of them, of course, was Tom Simmons, my old and dear friend who is seated here on my right. Tom, of course, was with the *Dallas Morning News* for his entire career I think, and that was the time that he had to come into play

---

[4]In fact, Yarborough did ride in the same car with the vice president, his political rival, because President Kennedy insisted upon it.

because the then managing editor was off on jury duty somewhere. And Tom as I recall, you were also out at the Trade Mart as I was at the time of the shooting, if that's not correct. Tom was one of the stalwarts in this market for many years. Why don't you tell us what happened down at the *Dallas News*, how you started getting ready for this thing and what happened when all hell broke loose.

Tom J. Simmons:[5] Of course, at the *News* this was a great day for our news staff and it was blemished of course by the

Simmons

famous one-page ad put in by Mr. Weissman,[6] welcoming Mr. Kennedy to Dallas in the most scurrilous terms you could imagine. And when we saw that ad in the paper, this kind of sent a shiver up our spine, and we wondered what we could do to play that down.

Of course, this is in the morning. And then Jean[7] and I and Jack Krueger's[8] wife went to the Trade Mart where the president was coming to address the luncheon. We were seated there, and nothing was going on. One of the service doors opened and I saw our photographer, Bill Winfrey, who is probably here this morning, come in and he was shaking like an aspen. I went over and said, "What's up Bill?" He said, "I heard on the police radio that the president has been shot."

And that was the first word into that auditorium of what had happened. I went back to table and told the ladies what I

---

[5] Assistant managing editor, *The Dallas Morning News.*

[6] Bernard Weissman had quickly put together an ad hoc committee, which he called the "American Factfinding Committee," for the sole purpose of placing the advertisement. He obtained donations from several right-wing Dallas businessmen, including the local coordinator of the John Birch Society, oilman Joseph P. Grinnan; H.L. Hunt's son, Nelson Bunker Hunt; and a trucking company owner who later would become the owner of the Dallas Cowboys' football team, H.R. "Bum" Bright.

[7] Jean Simmons, wife of Tom Simmons.

[8] Jack Krueger was managing editor of *The Dallas Morning News.*

had heard. The wife of the Methodist bishop Martin[9] was seated next to me, and her reaction was so amazing—she sort of sniffed and said, "You might have known it would be Dallas," or something like that. That was the immediate reaction of so many people, including a woman like her, whom I had never seen before or since.

But about that time the reporters who were covering the luncheon had come in and they were seated behind the head table, and all of a sudden just as on cue everyone of them sprang up and started running out the door, and I said well they got the word to them. Then an announcement was made from the head table of what had happened, and that immediately of course let us all go, so I caught a ride with this wild-eyed police reporter, Harry McCormick, and we drove over curbs—gosh, no thrill ride at Six Flags[10] has ever been worse than that. I told Jean to take the ladies home and I would be in touch later.

So we got to the *News* and, as Eddie mentioned, Jack Krueger was on jury duty in federal court, and he called shortly after I got there. He said he had gone out to look at the parade, and he had to go back to the jury room at 2 o'clock, but he'd be down there a few minutes after that as soon as the judge let them go. Meanwhile, Bill Rives and I, who were the assistant managing editors, were to see that things were shaping up. Of course, they shaped up automatically. Johnny King, the city editor, Tom Dillard[11] and the photographers, they knew what they were suppose to be doing without being assigned.

So I started making tentative decisions. You know how you do when the boss is out of the office. You do something and you hope when he comes back in a few minutes that it won't be wrong. So Bill and I marshaled our forces as best as we could, laying these tentative programs out, and we waited for

---

[9]William C. Martin, bishop in the Dallas-Fort Worth area, had been president of the National Council of Churches in 1952-53.

[10]Six Flags Over Texas, an amusements park mid-way between Dallas and Fort Worth at Arlington, Texas.

[11]Chief photographer, *The Dallas Morning News*.

Krueger and we waited for Krueger and we waited for Krueger so that he could come in and change things around. He came in at 4:30 and he was absolutely petrified. He said, Judge Davidson—this was old Judge T. Whitfield Davidson[12] who was still conducting trials after he was 90 years old. He assembled us after lunch and he said, "This is a sad day in the history of our nation, but jurisprudence must go on. Be seated, gentlemen, and continue the testimony." Well, you can imagine the jurors, the plaintiffs, the defendants, the lawyers, cooped up in a federal courtroom with something like that going on.

And when Krueger came, we of course had things pretty well going ahead. The decision was whether we should have an extra. Of course, the newsroom said yeah, we'll have an extra. What time? Give us a deadline and we will meet it. And it went back and forth. Shall we not. The circulation manager was there, ready to get the press crews started, ready to get people to take the extra out. You just don't print an extra and let it lie there in the building. This is an enormous project. And then finally the heads of the fourth floor, which was where all the executive offices were, they took a look at that ad and they took a look at what happened and they said it would just really not be good for the *News* to be coming out with seeming to profit by the president's death. So let's just forget about the extra, go ahead, we'll move the deadlines up early, as best we can, and go on from there.

And one of the brilliant moves that we made, and I don't know if it was Jack or Bill or me, was to tell Paul Crume that he was to write the lead story. You younger people might not know that Paul Crume was the front-page columnist at the *News* for 20 years and the sage philosopher of Lariat, Texas. He was the one most prominent personality that the *Dallas News* had, and Crume sat there chain-smoking cigarettes, sweating over his typewriter—no computer in those days, just

---

[12] Judge Davidson had been appointed to the federal bench by Roosevelt in 1936. Born in 1876 and reared on an East Texas farm, Davidson had been lieutenant governor of Texas in 1922-24 and president of the State Bar of Texas in 1927. He was widely known for his bombast and old-fashioned demeanor on the bench.

a plain typewriter—and he threaded together a beautiful story, and of course, right in the middle of it, things would happen. He'd get started; Oswald is shot. Then Tippit is shot. Then rumors about was it a conspiracy, this, that and the other. The LBJ swearing in. You could not have dumped a more complicated story on a writer and yet he managed it so beautifully that that was one decision that we made early and we made it right.

Barker: Tom, thank you very much for those remarks. We'll get back to you a bit later. Next to Tom is Russ Thornton.[13] Russ was at Channel 5, WBAP, in those days, KXAS-TV today, the NBC affiliate, and they had a unique problem because the newsroom was in Fort Worth and the film that we talked about—we had to shoot and go process and all—was over here in Dallas. So Russ, how did you manage?

Thornton

Russ Thornton: Pretty well, as it turns out. But before I get started, I just wanted to tell Tom that I also bummed a few rides with Harry McCormick, and we are both lucky to be here today. The role that I played was not all that significant, and I wish that Doyle Vinson[14] were alive today and would be able to be here with you because he's the one that made the early decisions and a couple of our people—Bob Welch and Jimmy Darnell—think you'll hear from later had direct contact with him early on. As most everybody can, well, as I look at some of these gray hairs around here, most of us can't remember what happened yesterday.

Barker: Folks used to call you "Red," remember?

---

[13] Producer of WBAP-TV's 10 o'clock news program, "The Texas News."
[14] Long-time news director for WBAP-TV.

Thornton: Yeah. It's kind of tough to look back 30 years, but I do remember when I first heard about this I was brushing my teeth, so I wasn't even at work. But the thing that I remember I guess most at the beginning of this thing was the planning that went into the coverage. NBC's Dallas guy then was a man named Moe Levy. Moe could just bug you to death, and he bugged us to death probably two weeks out on how are we going to do this, making plans. I really had rather he would have gone away, but he didn't. But basically he had a legitimate concern because of the problems that had occurred in Dallas earlier that there was quite likely going to be some kind of demonstration or incident or something out of the ordinary for a presidential visit.

So what we wound up doing is pooling our people with the network people. They brought in people. They also had some freelancers they brought in. So we had everybody placed everywhere you could think of, except the right place. As it turned out, the amateurs beat us with the pictures at the School Book Depository. At any rate, we had Love Field covered.

Of course, we had the other problem that the president was in Fort Worth that morning, and we had covered his speech at the Texas Hotel and his departure, and everything seemed to be in good shape. Most of us were out to lunch, and I wasn't even at work yet. My primary job was to produce the 10 o'clock news that night. At any rate, we thought we had everything covered well, and then it all went to hell fast.

When I left the house, I only knew that shots had been fired on the motorcade. I'm sure it wouldn't happen today, but it took me 10 minutes to get to the station and there was nothing on the radio about this in that 10 minutes. Time just seemed to drag. You know, give me some more information, and it didn't come. As I recall the same thing waiting on the AP and UPI wires. You just sat there and looked and nothing happened. I'm sure it didn't take very long; it just seemed like it took forever.

Barker: Speaking of that UPI wire, next to you, Russ, is Preston McGraw who did everything at UPI forever, and I was noting in his response to come here that he had written this great "hold for release" story about the speech in Dallas, so Mac, why don't you tell us a little bit about what UPI was up to and about that story and whatever happened to it?

Preston McGraw: It started in Fort Worth on Thursday night. In those days we always bulletined the president's arrival and departure. I went to Carswell[15] and did that, went

McGraw

to a telephone in a building on the edge of the runway and telephoned the arrival in. I wanted to go back after I had telephoned. The president's party had pulled up then. I wanted to go across the apron of the runway and see what was going on. A lieutenant stopped me, and he said, "You can't go there." I said why not, and well he said, "We're not allowing people to go across the field." And I told him I had to go and what I was up to, and he said, "I better go with you." I asked him why, and he said, "You might get shot otherwise."

Anyway, he took me over there, and I watched the goings-on until they left for the hotel. And then I went to the hotel, and the next morning I covered the speech to the Democrats, and at the same time I picked up the advance on the speech he was to give in Dallas. And I wrote an advance on it, hold for release, and sent that by telegraph and then I went on to Dallas. Meantime, Merriman Smith, who was the White House correspondent[16] who had gone on to Dallas—he was in a car right behind the president and Mrs. Kennedy—and I went on to the Trade Mart. And there was a flurry of activity, and it made me nervous, so I went to a phone we had in the lobby and called the office and asked what was going on. They said

---

[15]Carswell Air Force Base in Fort Worth.

[16]Smith, of United Press International, had grabbed a portable telephone in his media "pool" car in the motorcade, fought off other correspondents, and first reported that shots had been fired at President Kennedy. He won the Pulitzer Prize for his coverage of events on this day.

the president has been shot. I asked where could I do the most good, and they said Parkland Hospital, so I went to the hospital.

Barker: OK. And next to Preston is Buster Haas from the *Dallas News,* and I apologize Buster that we have your name spelled wrong there on the card. Tom Simmons called that to my attention early on. Buster, what kind of detail was going on there down at the *News* at the time? You were kind of in the nitty gritty down there.

R.E. "Buster" Haas:[17] Well, actually I think I might be here under false pretenses. I was the makeup editor at the *News* at that time, and that was my job that day. Tom did all the work

Haas

and told me what to do. However, I think I may have been one of the few editors that actually was at Dealey Plaza when the president was shot. My wife and son with his four Kennedy buttons that he was wearing that morning. We had gone down there that morning, and I had had about three hours sleep before that.

But one of the things that I remember most was all the type that we had to get in the paper that night. I think the instructions were get everything into the paper that is fit to print, every picture that is printable in the paper. We'll publish as many pages as it takes. It turned out—I think we started out with 46 pages. I think we wound up with 50, which was tremendous at that time, eight blank pages. But we weren't set up in the composing room. I mean they did a tremendous job of setting the type, but then didn't have a place to put it. So they were piling it on top of trays of type. On that day I was assigned to be picture editor. We did not have a picture editor at the time, so I was probably the first one in the history of the *Dallas News* assigned to be a picture editor. I finished the night as a makeup editor with another makeup editor, but the hardest

---

[17]Haas died of an apparent heart attack, age 70, March 24, 1996.

part for us was trying to find the type, being stacked up. We finally succeeded at about 4 o'clock in the morning. Finally we had some news.

Barker: How late was the final edition?

Haas: It was after 2 o'clock. We just went until we could get everything in, but the newsroom finished about 4 o'clock that night.

Barker: You know, I guess one of the most famous photos is the one of Lyndon Johnson being sworn in aboard Air Force One. And our next panelist sitting down is Dave Taylor of the AP photo division. Dave played quite a role in that picture being developed. Why don't you tell us about that, Dave?

David Taylor: Cecil Stoughton, who was the Army photographer accompanying the president, brought the film into our office along with some of the photographers that were

Taylor

with the president. We processed it. Since it was made by the Army, we had to pool it with UPI, so we made the prints and UPI sent a man over to pick up. We were there, trying to decide an off time. They had to get back. We wanted to transmit simultaneously. I had one phone talking with Jerry McNeill to see if he had gotten the picture yet and was ready to go. The other phone was our New York office screaming how much longer, how much longer. So finally Jerry got the picture and got his caption written; ours was ready to go, and we said OK, let's have it, and we both went at the same time. The picture moved all over the United States and from then on we retransmitted and retransmitted all over the world. And that kept on. After that, it was just pandemonium. Photographers went to police station, Texas Theater, and everywhere else, and it was just a constant running around from then on.

Barker: Well now you also got in on a little later on the Zapruder film.[18] You were one of the first people to take a look at that.

Taylor: Yeah, Harry McCormick came in and told us that the Zapruder film was going to be shown Saturday morning. We went up there, and it was UPI and *Time* and *Life,* Associated Press and maybe some others. We started the bidding on the film. I was on the phone to New York, our general manager telling me how much money I couldn't spend

Barker: How much did he authorize for the AP to spend on the film?

Taylor: It was $1,500, and I went back to our man to tell him. Mr. Zapruder said, "Well, *Time* and *Life* have already bought the film," and later on he said, "Just what would the AP have paid?" I said, "Mr. Zapruder, you'll never know."[19]

Barker: Thank you, Dave. Tom Dillard, who for many years told all those photographers down at the *Dallas News* what was in focus and what was out of focus, and Tom had quite a weekend both in the very beginning and as that weekend progressed. Tell us a little bit about it, Tom, if you will. You're on.

Dillard: Yes, I know, but I didn't know your question.

Barker: Oh, would you run the tape back? (laughter) No, no, no, I was just saying that you kind of told all those photographers down at the *News* what to do and how to do it, and so you had one big weekend of a lot of folks telling them what to do. Tell us a little bit about how that photography department operated that weekend.

---

[18] Abraham Zapruder was the Dallas dress manufacturer who took the famous 8 mm. amateur film showing rifle shots striking President Kennedy.
[19] Time-Life reportedly paid $250,000 for the exclusive rights to the film.

Dillard: Well, I didn't really tell everyone what to do.

Barker: Well, I'm kidding you a little.

Dillard: We had a rather peculiar situation. Most of the photo operation requests came through the various editors, especially the city desk. Before this thing developed, the Kennedy arrival, we assigned responsibilities to certain photographers. I personally had the president as my responsibility, while he was in Dallas. We had of course other people at certain locations. I was to get the arrival at Love Field and the parade and the luncheon. Those were my responsibilities, and it is important that the president's pictures were my responsibility.

So at Love, everything went fine up to the point that the  whole day became a great frustration for a photographic person. First thing, parades were usually handled with a flat-bed truck for pool and certain selected photographic personnel to ride in front of the presidential car in presidential parades. That was canceled at the last minute. We were put in Chevrolet convertibles to ride several cars back. I think we were about six cars back— Bob Jackson and I and a couple other boys were in this parade. That put us totally out

Dillard

of the picture.

The parade stopped once for Kennedy to go out and shake hands, out in North Dallas. And I tried to run up and get a picture there, but by the time I got there the parade had started again. So I was unable to do anything.

Then we arrived up on Houston Street, and the shots broke out—one shot, then two shots, then three shots. I immediately recognized them as rifle shots. Bob Jackson[20] said he saw a

---

[20]Bob Jackson was the *Dallas Times Herald* photographer who on Sunday, Nov. 24, took the dramatic photograph of Jack Ruby shooting Lee Harvey Oswald in the Dallas Police Department basement. Jackson won the Pulitzer Prize for his photo. His comments appear on pages 111-113.

rifle in the window on the upper floor. By the time I located it and got a wide angle shot and a telephoto shot, the rifle had already gone. Frustration.

I jumped out of the car, ran down to the corner. People were lying on the ground. I shot a picture or two there, saw that there was nothing for me there.

Jumped on the next car that came by, went out to the Trade Mart. People there told us that the presidential car had gone by. I went directly to the hospital. There was nothing at the hospital but some people trying to put the bubble back on the limousine. And from then on, it was problems. Photographically, we couldn't do anything. Bob Jackson and I discussed it last night, what great frustration it was. Bob unfortunately had unloaded his camera when the shooting started; he had no film, no way to shoot, for an early edition. But then of course, photographically we had Joe Dealey, our president at the *Dallas News*, in his generosity, turned over our morgue, our reference library, to all the visiting press. They were to get to receive pictures at our $2 a print fee. Of course, what happened, the press scavenged our reference library and took everything of any value, carried it off.

I stayed up quite late, and later on that evening we learned about the Zapruder film. Harry McCormick and I went out to the film lab, and I tried to talk Zapruder into letting me have a copy, letting me photograph a frame of his film, and Harry McCormick tried to con Zapruder into letting him be the representative of his film. Neither of us was successful. Course then it was back to the office and try to make some sense of the whole thing.

The next morning, Saturday, I went to [Dallas County Sheriff] Bill Decker's office and sat around there most of the day, trying to get a picture of Oswald being shipped down to the county, which is the normal procedure.[21] The powers that

---

[21]Persons arrested by City of Dallas police officers customarily were retained temporarily in a small, upper-level jail at the police station pending investigation, then transferred to the county jail in the Dallas County Criminal Courts Building after charges were filed.

be, Curry[22] and the others up at the police station, held back, because of pressure from the national media, I think. So Oswald never appeared at Bill Decker's shop. Someone came to the shop and told a television cameraman—Jim Underwood, who is dead now, I understand[23]—about a bullet mark on the curb, so Jim and I went down there and I took my pen out and held it for him to shoot a shot and then he held the pen for me to take a still shot. That didn't seem to show up very much, which seems to me to be a rather key facet of the first bullet theory, because it's very definitely a rifle bullet mark on the curb, directly in line the sixth floor of the School Book Depository, which we have the picture, and later events the media seems to have come along to my way of thinking that there was one gunman without conspiracy.

Barker: Thank you, Tom. Down there next to you is my old friend, Charlie Dameron. Charlie had probably a unique problem in that the *Times Herald,* which we know is no longer in existence, was the afternoon paper then, and to have this big event to take place at 12:30 when you had planned everything else, tell us what happened?

Charles F. Dameron:[24] Well, I think any of you out here who have ever toiled in the vineyards of an afternoon newspaper, a metropolitan newspaper, can understand the terrible problem we faced of covering an event considered very, very big. We rarely had ever had a president come into Dallas, if you think about it. Roosevelt came in way back and dedicated Lee Park.[25] A few things like that, but this was big doings.

---

[22]City of Dallas Police Chief Jesse E. Curry.

[23] Deceased, September 3, 1983.

[24]Charles F. Dameron was news editor of the *Dallas Times Herald.*

[25]President Franklin D. Roosevelt visited Dallas in June 1936 principally to attend the opening of the Texas Centennial Exposition. He also unveiled an equestrian statue of Robert E. Lee at Oak Lawn Park, at which time the park's name was changed to Lee Park.

Of course, we published four editions a day at that time, and we hit the streets in the morning about 10:30 with a street sale edition that would go out into the country also. Then about an hour later, we would follow up with a county edition. There were 28 municipalities in Dallas County in those days. We distributed a few papers to all of them. Then our first home delivery went to about a hundred thousand homes, and we decided of course as we started planning it that there was no way we could put a paper into the homes of people in Dallas that didn't have the president of the United States here and what he was doing.

Dameron

So we had a high-powered gathering of editors to plan all of this, and we decided well we would produce of course two editions—we couldn't very well stop that—and then we would just hold the presses, which was a most extraordinary thing at the *Dallas Times Herald* and probably at the *Dallas Morning News,* too. You know, production guys blanched at the thought of holding presses up for an hour to put a story. Anyway, we did that.

But I would like to sort of set the stage briefly. As an afternoon paper, you know, back thirty years ago, you mentioned you know our tools that we worked with—they were a little rudimentary compared to 1993. Reporters still wandered around with scraps of old copy paper that they had folded up and they took notes on it. They seemed to write stories just as well as the later reporters who had nice little notebooks. They came back and banged their stories out on old Remingtons and Underwoods, you know. They turned them in in "takes" as the deadlines approached on important stories. All of you know what a take was. You know you write two graphs and rip it out and holler copy and the copy boy would come pick it up. Then the editors would turn these stories or these takes over to the rim man on the old horseshoe desk—which Buster [Haas], you remember quite well—and some of those guys even wore the old black shades, the eye shades, and they were pretty good too.

And they used these very black pencils; I think they were number ones or whatever they were. They were black enough so you could scratch out and make a reporter's copy readable and accurate and grammatical and all of those good things. Of course, that doesn't happen any more because we've got the computers, which are marvelous, marvelous things. But then down in the composing room, you know you had all these other old guys with the eye shades who sat there with those clanking machines—we had about 40 of them in the composing room—and they would set type. They could set type very well when they had to. So anyway, we were all constrained, an afternoon paper especially, with time. How much can you produce? Linotype machines don't set type very fast, or did not. You had to go through stereotype. You had to go through all that business.

It took about 45 minutes for us to produce a zinc engraving to get in the paper. We didn't even have an engraving shop. Neither did the *Dallas News.* We farmed it out and had these little guys on bicycles who rode up and picked up these pictures and dashed down and bring the "cuts" back for the editions. Anyway, so the rigid schedules were a little frightening at times.

As we decided what we were going to do when the president came to town, we sat down and drew up and I finally put this thing together as news editor a meticulous operation, almost like a military operation, with the rather limited personnel resources that we had. *The Times Herald* in those days didn't believe in spending large amounts of money on extra reporters and editors. (Laughter) They didn't believe in paying lots of money to reporters and editors either. So we decided in light of what has been discussed before, the Adlai Stevenson event, John Birchism was fairly rampant in some areas of Dallas and North Texas. We were sort of scared, or a little apprehensive I guess, that some nut was going to do something stupid, like that matronly lady who slammed Stevenson in the face with that placard and spat at him, you know. That was real Dallas, wasn't it?

So I drew out this plan to station a photographer and a reporter at every major intersection on the route of the motorcade so that if something happened, we would have folks close by. We had two top reporters already riding with the president's press plane. Bob Hollingsworth was our Washington correspondent. He had been with the president, of course, all along and covered Fort Worth and so forth. We had two other reporters and a photographer we sent over to Fort Worth early in the morning on that fateful Friday to pick up sidebar stuff, etc., and to just be on hand there. They were to dash back over to Dallas by the time the president was dashing over to Dallas to Love Field and they would stay there at Love Field until the president departed later after the speech. We were trying to be sure we had bodies everywhere they needed to be placed.

We had six reporters and two photographers inside the Trade Mart building. Now I think Tom [Simmons] probably would back me up. When you got in there, you couldn't get out. That's the reason we put these people inside. Vivian Castleberry,[26] who probably will be here today, Vivian was one of the many people—there she is—who was there at the Trade Mart building. Then we had stationed a couple of reporters and photographers outside the building, so that they could at least be fluid enough. This was all just with the preparation.

Back in the office we beefed up a rewrite staff. We had a rewrite system in those days sort of modeled after the great Chicago newspaper rewrites. We put very experienced, fast writers, experienced people who could turn copy out by the ton, and we beefed it up to five people. We picked out the copy editors, or copy readers as we called them then, who each was assigned specific stories. We gave them the slug line. We were back in the Neanderthal ages. We had little old slip of paper we'd write the slug lines on so you could send it down to composing room. But we wanted to be sure we didn't have conflicting slug lines or we would wind up with the damnedest mess.

---

[26]Vivian Castleberry was women's editor of the *Dallas Times Herald.* Her comments are on pages 55-56.

So we were all ready to go and then of course all hell broke loose. But during that planning we decided that we must have a live picture of the president in the afternoon paper. Even though we were holding the press and whatnot and this was the good days, as you say, when cops and reporters and editors were real friendly, and we conned this guy, this motorcycle cop to bring some film downtown from Love Field so we could make that doggone edition. And here he comes roaring up, and we had somebody go outside and grabbed the film and souped it out. We also wanted to get some pictures in the later editions. We expected to probably produce a couple editions that afternoon, or three. We assigned Jim Featherston,[27] who is out here. Jim was our courthouse reporter and his main job, among other things, was to be out there as the photographers' press car passed and to get this film that was to be shoveled out to him. I think Jim will probably later tell you about that. It scattered all over the street, and by God, he had these rolls of film all over the place, and of course three or four minutes later the assassination took place and we almost forgot that stuff.

Barker: Charlie, we will be picking from the assassination on as we go on into the day. There was one thing that I wanted to get into. There was only one newspaper in the area here that did an extra. That was the *Fort Worth Star-Telegram.* I think Horace Craig is here this morning. Where are you Horace? Come up here and tell us if you will why the *Star-Telegram* decided to go with an extra and neither of the Dallas papers did. You're going to have to raise that mike, aren't you? Forgot you are over 8 feet tall. That's all right. Have at it.

Horace Craig: Well, I'm Horace Craig of *Fort Worth Star-Telegram.* At this time, I was assistant city editor, which means for $5 extra a week I would work all the other hours that nobody else wanted to work and on the days when they didn't want to come in. (Laughter) So that's why I was in the office that Sunday that Oswald was shot.

---

[27]Featherston's comments are on pages 48-50.

My first job that day was to go by the news stand and pick up all the out-of-town newspapers for the executive editor. This done, I was in the office alone with one copy boy who was cutting wire copy, and I was trying to figure out what I was going to do with my staff of two that was coming in later in the day. When my city editor's wife, Jean Hitch called, said she had been watching television, just saw Oswald shot at the station.[28] Well, that meant my quiet Sunday was shot also.

I immediately went to the wire room, and I checked and AP was moving a bulletin at that time. This was the case. I went to the phone and notified my editor, Jack Butler, began calling in the staff. We called in everybody on the staff, sent

Craig

half of them to Dallas, and I decided I better keep about half of them in the office because I was going to get flooded with a ton of copy here shortly. But this being Sunday, we didn't have an afternoon paper, and it was a long dry spell before our readers would really get anything in hand. So we decided early on that we would publish an extra this day. So our editor, Jack Butler, took on the chore of putting together the staff that we'd need. He called in the typesetters and the stereotypers and the pressmen, the copyreaders. He worked with circulation to make sure we could get the paper circulated. I forget how many papers we published, but I think we sold all of them that day.

Barker: I bet you did. Thank you, Horace. We appreciate it.

Craig: Jack Tinsley here?

Barker: Oh, is Jack back there? OK, thank you Horace.

---

[28] The city editor was Bill Hitch.

Jack Tinsley:[29] Eddie, one thing. We published two extras that weekend: one on Friday afternoon after the regular run and one on Sunday afternoon. Copies of both of them are over there in that display on the left side.

Barker: Great. Thank you very much, Jack.

Dameron: Say Eddie, before you close off, I know all of you probably see but I did bring some of the real honest front pages we managed to come up with late that afternoon.

Barker: What time did that hit the street?

Dameron: This hit the street about 2 o'clock. [Dameron displays the front page of the afternoon *Times Herald* bearing

the bold headline," PRESIDENT IS DEAD, CONNALLY SHOT."] We had to go and get what we use to call the big linoleum type to make a headline because the Ludlow machine

---

[29] Jack Tinsley was a reporter for the *Fort Worth Star-Telegram* at the time of the assassination. Later, he became executive editor.

wouldn't set anything above a 72 [point size], so we turned out about a 100,000 extra papers that afternoon over the normal run. We had to really put out three editions when you got through with it.

Barker: OK, thank you. We are going to try to keep this on time, and I think Darwin we are just about on time. Did you want to move on? Thank you, gentlemen very much. We'll have a big switch and move to our next panel.

At the Scenes:
The Motorcade,
School Book
Depository, and Trade
Mart

Hugh Aynesworth, Moderator

Some journalists were in the motorcade and others already were stationed at or near Dealey Plaza when shots were fired. Others were at the Trade Mart with a host of Dallas dignitaries eager to welcome President Kennedy. (This session began at 9:30 a.m. and ended at 10:30 a.m.)

Payne: So many memorable, unforgettable scenes we have from that Friday—among them the motorcade, Dealey Plaza, the Trade Mart. The moderator for our "At the Scenes" panel was at more key scenes than any other journalist. Hugh Aynesworth, then at the *Dallas Morning News,* was at Dealey Plaza when the president was shot. He was in the Texas Theater when Oswald was captured. And he was in the police basement when Ruby shot Oswald. No one else can claim all those distinctions, although Bob Jackson has two out of three of those.[1]

---

[1] Jackson was not present at the Texas Theater when Oswald was arrested, but he did hear the shots at Dealey Plaza and see a rifle protruding from the sixth floor window, and he took the historic photograph of Jack Ruby

It might not be surprising to know, considering his propensity for being at the right place at right time that Hugh Aynesworth already knew Jack Ruby before he shot Oswald. I might add that this wasn't all luck. For instance, I was with Joe Sherman, John Schoellkopf, and the late Paul Rosenfield[2] outside the School Book Depository when word came that an officer had been killed in Oak Cliff. What a coincidence, I thought. An officer killed shortly after the president was assassinated. No, I wanted to stay at the School Book Depository.

Well, Hugh Aynesworth immediately saw a tie with a possible connection to the assassination, and he took off for Oak Cliff and got there in time to see Oswald captured. Hugh has spent more time than any journalist investigating the assassination. In his work, he uncovered one sensational angle after another. The most memorable for me was his exclusive story detailing Oswald's Russian diary.[3] It ran on thousands of front pages all over the world, and it was a *Life* magazine cover story. Later, Hugh covered the Jim Garrison trial in New Orleans, gaining the district attorney's lasting enmity by writing for *Newsweek* that all was not kosher there in New Orleans.

Hugh has worked for both the *Morning News* and the *Times Herald*, for *Newsweek*, for 20/20, and now he is southwest bureau chief of the *Washington Times*. He has co-authored five books on true crime, perhaps the best known one being his book on the serial killer Ted Bundy. Hugh has been a finalist for the Pulitzer Prize four times, and he also has an SMU connection, I'm happy to say. We were fortunate enough a few years back to have Hugh teach reporting classes. Hugh Aynesworth.

---

shooting Oswald in the police basement.

[2] All of them were reporters for the *Dallas Times Herald*.

[3] The diary was excerpted first in Aynesworth's own newspaper, *The Dallas Morning News*. Its existence was not known to the public until Aynesworth published his exclusive story. The diary, referred to by Oswald as his "Historic Diary," contained sensational revelations such as Oswald's attempted suicide while in the Soviet Union.

Aynesworth: Thank you, Darwin. Good morning everyone. I'm going to get into this pretty fast because we don't have much time. We want to keep it on track here. I was a young reporter—well, not too young. I was in my 30s already—at the *Dallas News* when this tragedy occurred. I was not assigned. I remember that day everybody was excited. I had coffee with

two or three different groups, and everybody was assigned to do something at the Trade Mart or the Love Field or along the motorcade. Or to take pictures here, or to do that, or to jump on the White House bus or whatever. I felt a little left out. I was the science editor and the aviation writer. I wasn't assigned. I really felt left out. So went down and had coffee about three times that morning.

Aynesworth

Oddly enough, I saw Jack Ruby that morning. He came down and had breakfast at the *Dallas News* cafeteria about an hour before the assassination.[4] But I decided this was a special day and even if I wasn't involved, I ought to go watch it, so I went over to the area around Elm and Houston streets and was there when the three shots rung out. Three definite shots. Total chaos. I still have trouble putting it all together, how it happened. I recall glimpses and visions and things that happened. And I was in a helluva spot because I didn't have a pencil and paper. I reached in my pocket—no pencil, no pen. And I saw a young boy. This was probably fifteen, twenty seconds after the shots, and everybody was running and throwing their kids down or trying to get out of there. You didn't know where to go because the open area here and the buildings behind, you didn't know where the shots were coming, if there were more, how many people. You didn't know anything, so you didn't know what

---

[4]Ruby had gone to the newspaper to place weekend advertisements for his nightclub. Several employees at the newspaper saw him, and Ruby was still there when the shots were fired at the president at Dealey Plaza, five blocks away, although it has been claimed that Ruby was seen at Dealey Plaza .

to do. But I saw this young boy with an American flag. He was very young, and he had this American flag with one of these great big pencils it was attached to. So I grabbed that, gave him a couple quarters so his dad wouldn't whip me, and I took off. In my pocket, I had two envelopes I had not mailed: the gas bill and the electric bill. And that was my pad. And I interviewed people all over the place that day.

As Darwin said, I heard the call come in from Oak Cliff[5] and I jumped in a car with two Channel 8 [WFAA-TV] people and we ran like the devil to the Tippit scene, interviewed people there. From there, of course, we went a couple other places, and finally into the Texas Theater, where I got there just in time, a few seconds in time to see the people coming up the aisle, finally jumping on Oswald. But we'll get into some of that later stuff later. All the people on this panel have unique experiences about that day.

My first panelist here, Clint Grant, wonderful, wonderful gentleman and one of my good friends. He was [a photographer] at the *News* for many, many, many years— may still be for all I know. Are you, Clint? Still there? All right! Clint came all the way with J.F.K. from Washington and was in San Antonio, Houston and Fort Worth before he came here. I remember one story he told about how his luggage was on *Air Force One* and he called after the assassination and asked if he should go back with the body and they said no. So he had to really skedaddle it out to get his luggage off that plane. But Clint can you tell us a little about all the involvement, all the things that you saw that day?

Clint Grant: Well, I've condensed mine so we can read it in the interest of time. Leaving from Washington November the 21st with the president and the White House press, we visited San Antonio, Houston, arrived in Fort Worth at 2 a.m., November the 22nd. The following morning, we actually flew the short distance from Fort Worth to Love Field, if you can

---

[5] An area south of the Trinity River and not far from Dealey Plaza.

imagine flying from Fort Worth to Love Field.[6] My last shot at the airport showed the president, the vice president, Governor Connally, their wives, Erik Jonsson,[7] the chief of police, Secret Service men and *Air Force One* in the background. Then I hopped into the open Cadillac convertible with three White House photographers. We were the number two camera car behind the president.

Twenty-five minutes later as we turned the corner at Main and Houston, I heard three shots rang out. As we turned into Elm off Houston at the Houston [Texas School] Book Depository we saw the president's limo take off at high speed with Secret Service men scrambling to get aboard. Spread out all over the lawn were people protectively sprawling all over their children.

Grant

The driver of our car was a Texas Ranger from Austin. Neither he nor the other photographers were from Dallas or knew Dallas. I had to direct them. We went to the Trade Mart. No one there seemed to know anything except that the president was not there. I had been away from Dallas for over a week and thought maybe they had moved to Market Hall. We went across the street there, asked, and a custodian there said a limo and a police escort with sirens blaring had just passed. I said, "Uh-oh, they are headed for Parkland. Turn around." Of course, that's a one-way street there. We turned around, and we were facing the rest of the entourage.

After we finally straightened out that mess, we rushed to Parkland. There in the limousine's back seat was a bouquet of roses. After a long wait, L.B.J. came off and was whisked off. Figuring he was headed for his plane, I radioed the city desk to ask if I should go to Washington with the president's body. They said no, so I grabbed a cab, rushed to Love Field to

---

[6] A distance of approximately thirty miles.

[7] Texas Instruments executive, president of the Dallas Citizens Council, and laater mayor of Dallas.

retrieve my luggage. Original plans were to go on to L.B.J.'s ranch. Just as I reached the plane, Judge Sarah T. Hughes was coming off the vice president's plane. I just missed her swearing in the new president.[8]

Aynesworth: Thank you, Clint. I had two questions. One, did you get your luggage? Two, did the *Dallas News* pay your cab fare?

Our next speaker is Bo Byers. I didn't know Bo until years later. Bo had a long career with the Associated Press long before he joined the *Houston Chronicle,* which he retired from probably ten years ago. That day Bo was here. He had been in Fort Worth also. I believe you were on the White House bus, weren't you?

Byers: Right.

Aynesworth: Tell us what your remembrances are of that day.

Byers: OK, let me jump back to Fort Worth for just a second because it ties in with being in Dallas the next day. Late the night before in Fort Worth at the Texas Hotel, several

Byers

reporters, John Connally, Julian Read who was his p.r. man, and I think Mike Meyers—I believe it was—from Dallas were eating a late breakfast before going to bed. And Connally asked me, he said, "Bo, don't you have a poll coming out tomorrow on how Goldwater and Kennedy would run in Texas?" And I said yes. I knew that my editor had told him. And I said yes, we do have a poll coming out. And he said, "What does it show?" I said, "Well, you can read it tomorrow in the paper."

---

[8]U.S. District Judge Sarah T. Hughes, who had been appointed to the federal bench by President Kennedy, was summoned to Air Force One by her old friend Lyndon B. Johnson to administer to him the oath of office.

We went to the elevator, and as he was getting on the elevator, he turned around and he said, "Come on. You got that story with you, haven't you?" I said, "Yeah, I do." He said, "Give it to me." Well, kind of on impulse, I took it out of my coat pocket and gave it to him. This ties in to a story that Connally told me later, that Kennedy had asked him how he thought they would do in the next year against Goldwater as they were riding in the parade. And Connally told him, "Well, the *Chronicle* has a poll coming out that day." And Kennedy said, "Well, what does it show?" He said, "Well, it shows that it will be close, but that you could win it." Our poll actually showed Goldwater would have won it 52 to 48, which is fairly close. Kennedy had won in '60, 51 to 49 against Nixon.

With that background, I'm going to jump to Dealey Plaza. I was on the White House press bus. We were on Houston. I was looking across the plaza when we heard the shots. I remember three shots. I have always had a memory—as a matter of fact, I've had nightmares about it—of the sunlight on Kennedy, and the explosion, the car almost coming to a stop, almost to a dead stop, and then accelerating at tremendous speed, so I knew, by instinct, that he had been at least shot at.

We went to the Trade Mart because we didn't know definitely what had happened. We went to the Trade Mart, went storming in there, found out that he was at Parkland. I asked Bob Manning. He said, "Yes, he is at Parkland." "Is he dead?" He said, "Well, I don't know, but he was hit." I called my news desk and gave them that bit of information, gave them a first-hand story on my eye-witness account of the shooting at Dealey Plaza.

Went to Parkland. Mary Rice Rogan was with me; she was another *Chronicle* reporter. We grabbed a phone. We held that phone continuously until we got the statement from the doctor that the President was dead. I went outside. I saw [U.S. Senator] Ralph Yarborough leaving. I said, "Where are you going?" He said, "We are going to Love Field to see Lyndon Johnson sworn in." He was going with Earle Cabell and several other politicians. I said, "Can I go with you?"

He said if you can get into the station wagon in the back. So I crouched in behind the back seat, and we drove to Love Field. They gave us clearance to cross the field, instead of going around. We got over there. Of course, I could not get on the plane. I was standing on the Tarmac. I saw Judge [Sarah T.] Hughes get off the plane. I ran over and I said, "Judge Hughes, did you swear in Lyndon?" And she said, "Yes, Bo, I did."

I turned around, wondering where I could get to a phone. At that moment, a Southwest Bell telephone truck stopped, unloaded a portable telephone on the Tarmac. I stepped into it. And you know—"reach out and touch someone." They did. I dialed our number. The operator came on and said, "What number are you calling from?" And I looked and said, "There's no number on this phone." She said, "You can't call from a phone that has no number." I said, "Look, I'm with the *Houston Chronicle.* I'm trying to call my desk to tell them that L.B.J. has just been sworn in." She said, "I'll put you through."

And she did. And I don't have the extra that had that, but since extras have been mentioned, this was a story that day with the poll story here about how the race would come out. I don't have the first extra we put out for some reason. This is the second extra. We put out two that day. They had yanked the poll story luckily off the front page for the bulletin about Kennedy dying at 1 p.m. Then we had on Sunday, and I'll cut the story right here. They talked about trying to get people to put out extras.

When we were at Parkland, Connally had his first press conference that morning, and we had gone out there for that. As we left the press conference, I saw some reporters running down the hall. I said what's happening. They said Oswald has been shot and they are bringing him in here. I ran down to the doorway entrance where they were bringing him in on a stretcher. I looked down at him, and I said to myself, he's dead. He was very gray.

Mary Rice and I called the *Chronicle,* got a hold of someone there on a Sunday afternoon—I suppose it was still morning, but anyway—and said, "Look. Oswald's been shot. We've got to get out an extra." They said, "Oh, we can't call everybody in and put out an extra here on a Sunday afternoon." I said, "Look. Here's the guy that is supposed to have assassinated the president and now he's been assassinated. Let's put out an extra." I think they had to call the editor to get a decision on doing it, but they did. And we had two extras on the assassination of the president and an extra about Oswald.

I was there for about 10 days. I went home. I still have nightmares occasionally where I see that car coming almost to a stop and then accelerating and I wake up screaming.

Aynesworth: I can understand. I can understand. Our next speaker has no name card, but he has a lot to tell us. He's Tom Alyea. That's what it takes. Tom was with WFAA-TV at the time, and I don't know where all he was that day, but I know he was in the Depository shooting on almost every floor. And I know he was very many other places, too. Tom, fill us in.

Alyea: Well, a little background. First, the grunts in the TV business have to provide along the way. But anyway, I got the

Alyea

lead-off position from my assignment editor, Bert,[9] who coordinated the thing. I was to meet the president in Fort Worth. You don't meet the president, really. But he was four hours late. After midnight he pulled up in front of the Texas Hotel. The Secret Service people had all the news photographers, cameramen, and photographers—I'd like to bring that up right now. When you read about a cameraman or photographer, a cameraman is a movie camera. A photographer is a still, if that'll help you.

All right, the president comes in. Instead, when he gets out of the limousine, instead of walking into the hotel, he walks across the street. There's people over there. Our barricades came down. Every newsman said all the rules are gone. We

---

[9]Bert N. Shipp, the assistant news director at WFAA-TV.

follow the president. The Secret Service started bumping into one another, grabbing at us, running up along the side of the president, trying to get ahead of him, trying to discourage him from going into the crowd across the street.

He went in. We filmed this. He said a few words. Then he waited. That was Thursday night. That night a couple of us went to the Press Club. I was taking some shots inside. It might be a special feature, and if so I'll need some expansion footage.

There were about two, three fellows there that were sitting at a table. The reason I mention this is because of this FBI business and the Secret Service people in the Press Club drinking. There were these people. They were well behaved. I didn't know who they were. I shot them—with the camera, you understand. And the (inaudible) in the camera broke. Here's a newsman covering the presidential visit with a broken camera. Quickly, I borrowed one from our stringer.

I'll go through this quickly. It's boring, but it helps get the background.

The next morning, the same thing happened. When he comes down, instead of going to the breakfast, he goes over and meets the people across the way. And we all hustle over. Secret Service—they panic again, and he goes back and we wait on the camera and he flies to Dallas. We drive the news unit back to Dallas, and the fellow who was assisting me, Rick Jones and I, we were coming in Commerce. We were parked on Commerce Street inbound on the way back to WFAA with the film I had shot of the president in Fort Worth. Of course, I covered his speech and everything. Our assignment was over.

We were directly opposite of where the president was hit. If I had turned my head to the left, I probably would have seen the whole thing. I did not see it. I did not hear any shots. I think the first thing I heard was when the three radios in the news unit were blasting an excited voice yells through one of the radios that shots had been fired at the president—not these exact words—all units, around the presidential motorcade I suppose, Code Three to Parkland Hospital.

Aynesworth: Could you tell us how you got in to the Depository? I think that's so important, what you saw in there, and how you got in there, and how fast you got in there.

Alyea: I just arrived at that.

Aynesworth: Well, for the sake of time, let's arrive.

Alyea: All right, I'll speed up. So I heard this. I looked at Elm and Houston. I grabbed my partner's camera; mine was broken. Three rolls of film; that gave me 500 rolls of film; we got to hurry, I can't explain the other two right now.

I raced across. I see the people rushing around, running for cover. I film on the way as I cross Main Street and toward Elm Street. People are diving; people are jumping on top of kids. I think they are hit. And I'm looking for policemen; they are not around. One's running this way, one's running this way. Some people are running toward the railroad track. Some are running toward the monument area.

Is that fast enough?

Aynesworth: You're doing well.

Alyea: I better hurry up. I'll leave out a bunch of stuff, and we'll just get right—I thought there is nothing going on here. I remembered the Elm and Houston bit. I thought OK, I'll go to Elm and Houston. I go up there and there is a crowd of people up there. Couple of cops. One car. There's no action here. So I said the police have to be some place. Usually when somebody shoots the president of the United States, there is some kind of activity there. But where he was, there was none. One guy was looking up; I look up. I look up, following his gaze. I said, to myself, this is why there are no policemen. They are all in the building.

I rush to the building. I hit the door to the building the same time a fifteen—oh, I don't know. Kent Biffle[10] could probably

---

[10]A reporter for the *Dallas Morning News* who also was inside the Texas School Book Depository. See pp. 50-52.

give you a better idea because Biffle was crawling up my back as we went through the door. I heard a fellow say, "Shut the door. Lock it. Nobody in or out." I'm waiting to see if he [Biffle] heard the same thing, because I'm sure he will be talking. So Biffle and I were the only two newsmen in. Biffle had his pencil, and I had my camera. I followed the people up, the search team, up the elevators, fourth floor, fifth floor. We go around the fifth floor, all guns were out. Big burly guy, well not a big burly guy, one fellow comes up and says, "What are you doing here?" "Well, I'm with the press." "We don't want the press. Just get down.") I turned and walked toward the stairway with my camera down. Go around a couple boxes and fall in behind. I found out later he was some kind of a federal man. Now, whether he was Secret Service, I won't go into that.

Sorry. God, I didn't think I'd have to run through it this fast.

All right, on the fifth floor—I'm going to get questions on this—I was walking with this officer, plainclothesman, and we see a sack on the floor. And a Dr Pepper bottle. I said *fifth* floor. He hit it with his toe. Some chicken bones came out of it. (I'm not going fast enough.) Chicken bones came out of it and I was interested because it was the first thing so far that I had to shoot. So I got some close-up shots of the sack, the bottle and the chicken bones. He walked on, because at that time they were not interested in three-day-old dried chicken bones. Because they were looking for someone who was going to be shooting back at them at any second, they thought; we all thought.

I run to the window—I walked to the window. It was open, and I shoot down and get pictures of the newsmen that were locked out, waiting to get in. The police officers who were arresting people and carting them off. Then joined the team again; there was nothing but the chicken bones, dried chicken bones, on the fifth floor. Then we went up to the sixth floor. We get up there, I don't know, maybe about a minute and a half, something like that.

Fellow said, "Captain Fritz and everybody come here." We walked over there. The fellow—you know his name. I won't go into it—he found the barricade and the open window with the boxes in the window. And I filmed the barricade, and I filmed the boxes in the window, the way they were before anybody touched them.

The boxes were placed in a particular, very interesting way that alters a lot of people's concept because these were the only pictures that were ever recorded of the way the boxes were actually placed in the window. Because before our friends downstairs with the still cameras and other cameras were allowed into the building—shall I stop?

Aynesworth: I was going to ask you if you saw the gun. Do you actually see the rifle and shoot it?

Alyea: Yes. That's more interesting, I guess, than the boxes, isn't it?

Aynesworth: A little bit.

Alyea: Yeah. Any way, they tore up the arrangement in dusting for finger prints, stacked them on top of one another. So pictures you see of the barricade and all this—the barricade was torn down. From the barricade, you could not see the window. But, all right. We secured that floor, went to the seventh floor. Nothing there. We went to the roof. And for those who are going to ask a question, no, there was no rifle on the roof. There was no rifle on the roof; we looked everywhere. We came back down to the seventh floor. We re-searched the seventh floor. We were tracing our steps.

Aynesworth: Tom, forgive me. I'm going to have to stop you because we are going to have to leave some room for some questions. You've brought up some things that probably people will want to ask some questions. So let's have some time for those.

Alyea: All right, I'll just stop and maybe we'll talk about finding the rifle later.

Aynesworth: Thank you. All right. I've have some questions. Our next speaker on the panel was a reporter for the *Dallas Morning News* who I think was probably with three other reporters, the closest press people to the president when he was shot. Mary Woodward was her name then; it's Mary Woodward Pillsworth now. She comes from a suburb or very close to Albany, N Y. And I remember Mary's story, what she came back and wrote that day. She came back, incidentally, and said, "The President is dead," and a lot of people didn't take her serious because she was excited, as we all were. Well, I'll let you tell it, Mary:

Mary Woodward Pillsworth: Well, first of all, I'm very happy to be here as a representative of my gender. (Laughter, applause) You may notice on your list of

Pillsworth

participants that I am an addendum, and that's rather descriptive of my role on that day as well. I was young, as we all were then, and fairly new in my career, working in women's news as most women did then. So I didn't really have a role to play in that day, but I had always been very politically active. And I had met the president actually on several occasions prior to that, having even attended the Democratic National Convention.

But I had never met Jacqueline Kennedy, and I was so excited that I would have my first chance ever to see Jacqueline. So I decided I was going to walk down on my lunch hour and watch the parade, regardless. And I talked three of my friends from the women's news department into going with me. We took some bag lunches, and we were just going to sit and wait for the parade.

Well, we were going to stop right in Dealey Plaza on Houston Street, but it was a little crowded there and crowds were thin over on Elm Street. So we walked across to Elm and stationed ourselves just down from the School Book Depository Building and waited for the parade to come by. And we were chatting, and as we were talking, I looked up at the grassy knoll. And I said to my friends, "That's a very dangerous looking spot to me. It must be, there must be a lot of security up there because it looks like a perfect spot if somebody wanted to do something."

And then the motorcade came along. I couldn't believe it; finally, I'm going to see Jacqueline Kennedy and she is looking in the other direction. So I yelled and I said, "Please look this way." And they looked right at us, waved, and at that moment I heard a very loud noise. And I wasn't sure what it was at that point, and I turned to my friends and asked, "What was that? Is some jerk shooting off firecrackers?" Then I heard the second one, and this time I knew what had happened because I saw the president's motion. And then the third shot came very, very quickly on top of the second one. And that time, I saw his head blow open, and I very well knew what had happened by that point.

But what I couldn't really believe, as someone else mentioned, was the car, after that first shot, had come practically to a stop. Later on, looking back on it, I said I could not believe how well trained Secret Service people reacted so slowly. I would have expected that from ordinary human beings, but I expect that they would have reacted much quicker.

This I always felt in my mind, I knew the first shot missed. I have never waivered on that. I see know that is getting a lot of support. I said that from Day One, that the first shot missed. I never changed my mind on that. I felt the second shot was not a mortal blow. I felt that had there been proper reaction time that the man might still be alive today. But immediately after that, we waited for just a few minutes on the street corner, kind of gathering ourselves, and walked back to the *Dallas Morning News*.

And when I got, we walked in, I met my supervisors, and I kept saying, "The president's been killed. The president's been killed." And nobody really wanted to believe me. My friends who were with me would not even support me in that. They were saying well, something happened. He's been shot. There's been shooting. But nobody was willing to say, "They've killed him." But I kept insisting, "He's dead. I know he's dead, or else I hope he's dead because his head's blown open."

Eventually they started to take me a little seriously. I guess some other reports were coming in, and they said, "Well, please write it down. Sit down and write it down."

So I started writing the story, and I wrote exactly as I knew it from that moment without having talked to anyone else, without being influenced by any outside people. I wrote it as I saw it. And to this day I think I wrote it correctly. I read it again for the first time, just in preparation for coming here. And I said in that story that there were three shots. I said that there was a pause between the first and the second one. I said the first shot did not hit anything, and I believe that very strongly to this day.

The only thing that I guess I got myself in a little bit of controversy about, I said that the shots appeared to have come from behind me and to my right. And I did say "seem to." I didn't say they *did* come from that direction. Because, first of all, I have very great difficulty determining the direction of sounds anyway. I'm the kind of person on the throughway when I hear a siren I panic because I don't know where it is coming from.

And secondly, I had spoken to my friends just prior to the event, suggesting that the grassy knoll would be the perfect spot for an assassin, so I said it was somewhat like self-fulfilling prophecy, that when it happened, I naturally expected it to have come from where I had predicted it would come from. So in reality, I do believe they did come from the School Book Depository Building.

So I get a little bit upset when I get put in the other column. But it may be very interesting to a number of people, including people like Mark Lane and Jim Garrison who repeatedly tried to contact me and raise the question of why I was not called before the Warren Commission and the reason why, of course, is because I had said the shots had come from the other direction, but in reality, I never spoke to either of the gentlemen, although they have both indicated, including Mark Lane in the Warren Commission, that he had spoken to me. But I never spoke to Mark Lane in my life, except to say I wouldn't speak to him.

Aynesworth: Sometimes that's enough.

Pillsworth: I guess so. We learn hard, don't we? Just a little concluding thing. At the end of that day, I went home at my regular time, but we were all so keyed up that I decided that I had to go back to the office. So I went back that evening. And as a journalist's perspective, it was just amazing. It was like when I was growing up and wanting to be a journalist, it is what I thought journalism was going to be like, with this city room of people yelling copy boy and running back and forth and bells going off and that's just like it was that night. And there were people from all over the world there, and I stayed on all night long. I spoke Spanish, so I was translating for people, and I was running copy. And from that was another very interesting and exciting aspect of being a journalist on that night, and I don't know if we'll ever see something like that again, but it was truly like the movies. I felt I was back in "Front Page."

Aynesworth: Thank you, Mary. I hope we will never see anything like that again. Our next panelist, Bill Winfrey, who was at that time a *Dallas Morning News* photographer, Bill was all over this story. He was all over it. I don't know where he was that day. I know I ran into him. I ran into him and went with him on the other days. Bill, tell us your story.

Winfrey: First of all, I was assigned to cover the luncheon. I was given this set of credentials, the invitation from the Dallas Citizens' Council, the Dallas Assembly and the Science Research Center.[11] I think we forgot who put on the luncheon.

---

[11] These three organizations were the official sponsors of President

"Request the pleasure of the company of Mr. Bill Winfrey at a luncheon in honor of the President and Mrs. Kennedy, the Governor and Mrs. Connally . . ."

Aynesworth: Bill, you can't read all those names. I'm sorry.

Winfrey: But anyhow, without this, you didn't go near here. All the photographers and reporters were given these

Winfrey

credentials, and everyone I've talked to has thrown theirs away. These hanging tags? Jerry's [McNeill] got his, OK. This press tag you had to have on hand on you to get around. I went to the Trade Mart, set up my cameras, waiting for the president to get there and walked down to talk to Deputy Chief [George L.] Lumpkin, who was in charge of security there.

When they came by, they went by at a high rate of speed. You could see people hovering in the back seat. The Secret Service hanging around, you know, the motorcycles. They went right on by.

We then found out from Deputy Chief Lumpkin that he had been hit twice. We did not know with rocks, bottles, guns, whatever. I went inside and found Tom Simmons, Joe Dealey, the president of the *Dallas Morning News* at that time, John King, Bill Rives, the people I worked for and told them what had happened. Asked to be relieved of my duty. I had an assignment. We followed blindly. I picked up Tom Milligan, the farm editor. This is a good point and case for journalism. The farm editor came with me to help. He carried my camera bags, an extra camera, and helped shield me.

Kennedy's visit to Dallas. The Citizens' Council was an organization of leading businessmen who for years had been a behind-the-scenes force in Dallas affairs. The Dallas Assembly was the "junior" organization for future members of Citizens' Council, and the Science Research Center, an institution tied closely to Texas Instruments, Inc., was a forerunner to the present University of Texas at Dallas.

I want to take a little bit of time here, because this is pretty important. When we got to Parkland Hospital, I had to park way around, but I knew where emergency was. I'd been there before. As I ran around the building—and all you photographers will appreciate this—I had a 400-millimeter lens with a new gadget called a follow-focus. You squeeze it to focus the camera. It looked like a bazooka or an Uzi.

The Secret Service immediately run up and put guns to me and Tom's head, made us lie on the ground, and looked at my camera. So we could have been killed out there, too. But we went around and I made pictures of Jackie when she walked out of the hospital, Mrs. Cabell[12] sitting alone in a car, the roses laying in a pool of blood in the thing, and they came out and said we are going to have—and all of the hundreds of people that were kneeling and praying around the hospital.

Malcolm Kilduff[13] held a press conference right after that, and he said, "The president is dead." By the, we had Washington, Austin, Mike Quinn, Bob Baskin,[14] all these people in the press corps that came in. I took all these people in my car back to the *Dallas News*. Tom Dillard was on foot. He had been riding in the presidential motorcade. So they all piled into my car, about seven of us, I think. I had two-way radios.

We started back to the *Morning News*. Interesting footnote—we had to stop. Bob Baskin was a basket case. He came apart. We stopped. Tom Milligan bought him a bottle of whiskey. We never told Bill Rives that. I believe the man, he was hyperventilating, the man would have died. We saved his life. What can I say?

Anyhow, but as we got a few blocks from the *News*, on my police radio—we came right through Dealey Plaza on the far side, coming east—they said a policeman had been shot in

---

[12]Dearie Cabell, the wife of Dallas Mayor Earle Cabell.

[13]Kilduff was the acting presidential press secretary for the presidential visit because Press Secretary Pierre Salinger was en route to Tokyo.

[14]Quinn and Baskin were *Dallas Morning News* reporters.

Oak Cliff. Somebody on the radio, as I remember, told us that they thought there was a connection between the assailant.

I dropped off Dillard to go take charge of photographers, Baskin and Quinn and all of the gentlemen. Bob's dead now, but I'm sure Mike's here this morning. And Milligan. But, I went over there and as I got a half a block from the Texas Theater, here come the police in a throng, pushing somebody out the door and pushing him into a car. I turned and crossed over the median strip, turned around and beat the police to the police station, parked my car second lane out from the curb. They impounded it. The *Dallas News* did not pay for that.

But I rushed upstairs, where I was able to make this picture when Oswald came off the elevator. [Winfrey begins to display a series of photographs.] And Ferd particularly likes this picture here; I have him—I know, right though there. Then I made this one as they went down through here. This one I made later on with Ruby. This one a made during the trial of Marguerite. I took her out of the corridor; and we went and had lunch. And we went over and I posed this one there. Photographers are always scheming about something.

Aynesworth: Bill, we're going to have to move on. We are running a little bit late.

Winfrey: Well, that's about it. I stayed there all evening. That night Jack Ruby was in the hallway. I can't remember why. Hugh Aynesworth and I knew him, and everybody has all these strip clubs up and down through there.

Aynesworth: We're going to move on right now.

Winfrey: In talking with him, as I remember, Jack Ruby was the one that broached the idea of sending out for food. I do know that Pete Lucas of Lucas' B&B[15] brought two big trays

---

[15] A popular restaurant on Oak Lawn Street.

of food, the sandwiches and the ham and the turkey that we ate. Jack was like all of them. We were dumbfounded.

Aynesworth: I'm going to get the hook now, Bill. Thanks very much. But we do have to move. We've got several people to hear from. Our next panelist, Jim Featherston, was a courthouse reporter for the *Times Herald* that day. Jim was all over the place. He interviewed people at the scene, witnesses that day, including a couple of controversial situations. Would you tell us, Jim? He's now at Baton Rouge, teaches at LSU.

Featherston: That day I was at the corner of Main and Houston streets. That was shortly before the president was killed.

Featherston

There's a picture made, by the way, of me and it is in the background, and the Associated Press said this was made a minute before the President was assassinated. I heard the shots, but honestly I didn't recognize them as gunshots. I thought they were firecrackers. So I wasn't counting. If somebody asked me today how many shots I heard, I would say at least three.

At any rate, I ran down on Dealey Plaza. I talked with two women, Mary Moorman, who had taken a Polaroid picture, and Jean Hill. I got there. I wanted that picture. Period. At that time, I thought that was the only such picture in existence. So Mary Moorman agreed to give me the film.

I asked both of them to come back to the press room with me, which they did. I interviewed them. I called the rewrite desk. I really don't know who was on the rewrite desk. But they gave a, in their own words, they told what they had seen, and what they had seen was the president shot about 10 feet in front of them.

I'm going to dwell on this just a minute, because later on Jean Hill told the Warren Commission I went down there and I grabbed her and Mary Moorman, she was crying. That I wouldn't let her go. And I took them to a strange room. Of course, that was the courthouse press room. (Laughter)

Aynesworth: *That's* pretty strange.

Featherston: It *was* a pretty strange room, wasn't it? By the way, there was about half a dozen of us graduates—John Schoellkopf, Bob Welch, Jimmy Darnell, Darwin Payne. [Someone suggests "Jim Lehrer."[16]] Yeah, but Jim Lehrer is not here today. I'm talking about people that are here today.

Well, at any rate, she also said I told them that they couldn't leave and told them that I wouldn't let them stay and so forth. This is all nonsense. But that was about the extent of my activities that day. We had an old bottle of Thunderbird wine in the press room. Some lawyer had given it to us as a joke. He didn't think we were low enough to drink Thunderbird. (Laughter) But I drank every bit of it that day. (More laughter.)

Something else I'd like to talk about along that line. It involves several people here: Charlie Dameron, for one, and Darwin Payne, for the other. The first time I met Darwin Payne was when the prisoners escaped during the trial, the Jack Ruby trial. And I called up the *Times Herald* and told them five or six prisoners had escaped. And I'm sure Charlie thought I was drunk, so he sent Darwin down to check up on me.

Of course, I've interviewed Marguerite Oswald. I tried to interview Robert Oswald, the brother. He wouldn't talk to me. And I covered a lot of the Ruby trial. There is something else I wanted to say and I can't think of what it was at the moment.

Aynesworth: Well, if you think about it, we'll come back to you.

---

[16]Jim Lehrer, now host of Public Television's "NEWSHOUR with Jim Lehrer," who was a reporter for the *Dallas Times Herald* at the time of the assassination.

Featherston: Let me say one thing about all these conspiracy theories. I think that Hugh Aynesworth knows more about the assassination than anybody. Did Walter Cronkite say that one time?

Aynesworth: Oh, he said a lot of things.

Featherston: Let me say one more thing. Like a lot of people, I'm not completely satisfied with the Warren Report, but we were never able to come up with anything better, and I don't think we ever will.

Aynesworth: Thank you, Jim. Our next panelist is Kent Biffle, who was then a reporter with the *Dallas [Morning] News* and now is a columnist for the *Dallas News*. In between, he worked with me for a while at *Newsweek*. Kent was in the motorcade that day and I know he was in the School Book Depository Building. Tell us a little about it, Kent.

Kent Biffle: I feel like kind of a truth squad following Tom Alyea. No, actually, he set the scene pretty well in the School Book Depository Building.

We went in with the first wave of policemen. They immediately sealed off the building, and so we had it all to ourselves for the first—I don't know—two or three hours after the assassination. We got really tired of looking at each other.

But there were some things going on, of course. The crime lab people were investigating, and I remember I was worried when we first went in. I was afraid that a policeman was going to shoot me because

Biffle

these guys all had their guns out and they were nervous. I remember once stepping out of an office where I interviewed some office workers on the second floor. And there was a policeman at one end of the hall and another at the other end of the hall, and they both had riot guns and they both drew down on me when I stepped out in the hall.

But I never worried much about the assassin because I kind of had a theory that with the last shot he had killed himself, and they would find the body there in the building somewhere. And, in fact, when one of the detectives yelled at Captain Fritz,[17] "Over here," well I thought that they had finally found his body, but it was the rifle that the detective had found. You could see part of the muzzle and part of the butt plate sticking from under a box of books there.

And then a little later an officer came in and told Captain Fritz, "We've got a man down in Oak Cliff." They didn't immediately link this up with the assassination. It was like an altogether isolated incident. I recall that they reacted; they said his name is Tippit. At first, you know, they were all cast down because there was apparently an extroverted policeman named Tippit that they all knew and liked. And they were kind of relieved to hear that it was not him but the other Tippit who had been killed. Apparently J.D. was a quiet sort of man, and he was not well known to these detectives.

Then a little later, Roy Truly, the manager of the School Book Depository Building, came in and announced that one of his workers[18] had not reported back after lunch, and his name was Lee Oswald. And so things kind of dragged along.

After awhile, I decided I better get back to the office and write a story. By then, I was told I could leave the building, but I couldn't get back in. So Tom and I kind of enjoyed the exclusive story about as long as we could, but I had to get back to the office to write. I began walking back to the *Dallas Morning News,* and that name began to sound familiar. Lee Oswald? Lee Oswald? And then I remembered three or four years earlier, I had been working at the *Fort Worth Press.* The old *Fort Worth Press.* And had written several stories about

[17] Captain Will Fritz was the chief homicide investigator for the Dallas Police Department.

[18] Truly had hired Oswald on Oct. 15, 1963, after a friend of the Oswalds, Ruth Paine, had called him and said that she knew a "fine young man" with a wife and baby who needed work "desperately."

this Marine who had defected to Russia. I had interviewed his brother, and I had interviewed his mother. His name was Lee Harvey Oswald. And I snapped, you know. But by the time I got back to the office, Lee Oswald had been identified by the wire stories and everywhere, so that exclusive didn't last very long.

Any how, after that the days all kind of ran together. I still have difficulty sorting them out because it was one of those—as newsmen you have all been on stories like this, where you roll out of bed in the morning, put on your shoes and they are still warm.

Aynesworth: Thank you, Kent. Thank you very much. Now another gentleman without a name tag, and that doesn't mean he isn't important, his name is Bob Welch, and he's been a do-everything for WBAP-TV and Radio for many, many, many years. How many years, Bob?

Welch: Since 1960.

Aynesworth: Since 1960. Everywhere that I went during the assassination, I'd either see he or Jimmy Darnell.[19] They were everywhere. Tell us a little bit about it.

Welch

Welch: Well, Jimmy and I were actually at Love Field starting our day for Kennedy's arrival. We were there when he arrived, and Jackie was beautiful. And the president was handsome and young and red-headed, and he had a green and white striped shirt and looked like a yuppy more than a president. Of course, we didn't know them as yuppies then.

I was very, very impressed with this Democratic president. And I was very

---

[19]Darnell also was a reporter-cameraman with WBAP-TV. His comments are on pages 66-68.

pleased to be there recording this event. I filmed his going up and down the line of people, shaking hands with everybody. Everybody was very cordial, very supportive of the president. And he was very receptive to it all. He got in his car with Jackie and the entourage, Governor Connally and Nellie Connally. I was right there on the periphery of the car, shooting that, about as close as you can get to a president without getting whisked away. I was very pleased to have that position. A lot of the film that's on the air these days, that's the film that you see. There were other photographers there, but we all think that film was our film. And some of it was.

He drove off, and I was elated to succeed there at the airport, but my job was then to go to the Trade Mart. Jimmy [Darnell], in turn, was getting in the car to follow the president. There was only two of us. Eddie Barker earlier had said there were 34 people, or whatever, at KRLD, and we may have had that number at WBAP, which is now KXAS, but for all practical purposes, for WBAP there were four warm bodies. There was Jimmy Kerr, who is no longer with us. He was wonderful and our [Dallas] bureau chief and gave us the leadership there. There was Jimmy, and there was Dan Owens. Is Dan here? Is he here? Oh, thank you! I'm so glad he is here. He was one of the four. There was only four of us. And myself. There was really only four people covering the biggest story. That's why we are all here today, which I think is rather interesting. Later on, as the story moved on, of course more people became involved. But for all practical purposes, there was four of us in the game plan here in Dallas, and Dan Owens certainly is one of them.

So anyway, I went to the Trade Mart after the arrival, and everything was fine. I was excited. I had my position. I was supposed to film his arrival at the Trade Mart. I'm standing next to a squadron of motorcycles, long line of motorcycles, outside the main entrance of the Trade Mart. From out of nowhere comes in a very loud, as it was related to you early, comes this message: "There's been a shooting in the motorcade." Horrible message for a young man; I was 27 at the time. Listening to this in disbelief.

About the same time that I'm hearing this and trying to grasp what's happening, standing next to these motorcycles, I'm hearing these sirens coming down Stemmons and turning on to Harry Hines Boulevard in front of the Trade Mart. I see it, and as I see it, I react to it. I run toward a news car which is maybe a 150 feet from where I am. I was credentialed and able to be there and park. And as the car was passing and I was watching the car, I could see Jackie hunched over the president. I couldn't see the president, but I could see Jackie in her pink outfit bending over, so I knew he was hurt.

I didn't see the assassination, because I was at the Trade Mart. Jimmy [Darnell] was in the motorcade and shot that business, but I knew we had a problem. I got into the news car, and instinctively I pulled out of the parking lot of the Trade Mart. Parkland was about a mile or two from where we were, and I pulled in behind the president's limousine, if you can believe that, but I did, out of pure ignorance more than anything else. I just knew I had to get where the problem was. And I later learned in the Warren Report, although I've never saw it, I have heard from some sources, that one of the FBI fellows in the motorcade there was concerned about this car. They couldn't see the WBAP-TV [logo] because it wasn't in the front; it was on the side. So they were looking back at me, and they were concerned about this car that was much too close to the Kennedy's car, to the limousine and the bank of officers. And the message was, "Should we rub him out?"

Aynesworth: Bob, I hate to interrupt, but do you have a final thought or two? I think we are going to have to move. We are already late.

Welch: Well, that's fine.

Aynesworth: Thank you very much. I have two other people I want to call from the audience just for brief remarks. One is Vivian Castleberry. She was the woman's editor, I think, or at least was the woman reporter at the *Times Herald* at the time. She pressed all the barriers and all the limits and has done so many things I can hardly describe her, but Vivian has a couple of stories she wants to tell. Vivian.

Vivian Castleberry: Well, number one, I want to say that everybody who had anything to do with covering the story at one time or other thought they had an exclusive. And so it is nothing unusual for all of you up here to think you had an exclusive.

Castleberry

The second thing that I want to do is to say that I was at the Trade Mart that day. I was interviewing people as they came into the luncheon. I interviewed Judge Sarah Hughes when she came in, and I recall vividly—all of you who ever interviewed Sarah Hughes know what a master of understatement she was.

So when she got there that day and I interviewed her, I recall vividly that she said three things. One, that it was a great day for Dallas. Second, that she had been gravely concerned about the president visiting Dallas. And third, that she would be glad when he left Dallas. So I wrote those things down in my reporter's notebook, scribbling on an envelope as most of the others of you did, and then I called her that afternoon at her home right after she had sworn the president in and she gave me one of the first interviews that she gave. And again she was a master of understatement: "It's no big deal, he was my friend, they called and asked me to come and I went."

The second thing that I would like to do is to corroborate in detail everything that Mary [Moorman] said to you. Because when I got back finally at 3 o'clock that afternoon at the paper, it was bedlam and it was organized chaos at the *Times Herald*. But about between 3 and 4 o'clock, I had a telephone call from a first cousin. And her first words to me were, "Today I saw the president die." And I said, "Peggy, don't say another word until I put a piece of paper in my typewriter." And she quoted to me almost in exact detail what Mary has already told you.

The interesting thing was that Peggy Burney was Abe Zapruder's direct assistant, and so far as I know, her name appeared in a lot of the follow-up, but so far as I know, she was never interviewed by the Warren Commission. She was standing next to him when he told the famous film and was holding some of his camera equipment even while he did it. I thought that was a fascinating detail that maybe you would be interested in.

Aynesworth: Thank you, Vivian. James "Ike" Altgens, well known photographer for the AP, shot a very memorable picture that day, among others I'm sure, but it became very controversial because as I recall, and I do recall, it showed a man that looked like Oswald in the door of the Depository building, a fellow named Billy Lovelady, I believe. Ike, could you tell us a bit more about that?

Altgens:[20] The Associated Press has a rule. The rule is if you are going to write a story, make it short, and I've got five hours of copy I could give you, but I'm going to try to condense

Altgens

it to three minutes. I'm going to omit some things that you have read. I have already testified to the Warren Commission, so chances are you have picked that up there.

But there is an essential part to this entire sequence of events that I have personal touch with that I think you will find to be very interesting. I had already made a snap shot up at the corner of Main and Houston, and I came on down to position myself in a position where I could make something of a little bit better picture, close up. I had already also made a picture at the time of the first shot that I heard. I made a picture, you probably have seen it, where John Kennedy is grabbing his throat. Then I had positioned myself

---

[20]Altgens and his wife were found dead in their home on December 12, 1995, apparent victims of carbon monoxide poisoning. Altgens was 76.

in a way that I had already prefocused to the middle of the street from where I stood at the curb level—15 feet. That was on the scale, so I'm not exaggerating. That's the way it showed on my camera. As the progression of the unit came down, and it got very close to me, and I was prepared to make the picture—I never took it. I don't know if you've ever been pressured. I don't know if you've ever been startled. I don't know if you've ever been shocked to that point that you just sort of get glassy-eyed. But this man, his head when it exploded, sent a signal to everybody that there was a gun being fired from some source. And when the fragments came over, and some of it falling at my feet, it was for very, very real. I did recover enough in time to make a picture of the Secret Service man going up to, over the deck lid in order to bring Jackie Kennedy back inside the car.

I had a call from a woman. She says, "What is your remembrance about Jackie Kennedy being on the back of that limousine?" I said the woman was scared out of her mind and she was looking for a way to escape. "Well, that's not the way I heard it. I thought she just went out there for some fresh air." I think you can recognize that under conditions like this, you are not going for a stroll even if it is crawling around on the deck lid of an automobile.

Now pay attention to this, because this is very important. I've had so many people coming to me about cross-fire from the knoll and from the other areas. When John Kennedy was hit by this bullet that obliterated that back of his head, and it did come from the rear, there's no question about it because the movement of the body, and I didn't realize at the time he was wearing a back brace that held him in position and he was already tilted from the earlier shot toward his wife. So when he got the blast from the rear, that released his being caught into that cushion and he continued to fall in that position, right into Jackie Kennedy's lap. But here is what's important. As John Kennedy was falling down into Jackie Kennedy's lap, there was no blood on the right hand side of his face. There was no blood on the front of his face. But there was a tremendous amount of blood on the left hand side and

at the back of his head, which suggests to me if someone was
shooting from any other position, there would be evidence in
that particular area because they didn't find any body blows
from bullets and shrapnel that could have been somewhere
else, that could have come from that direction. It's all a
hypothesis. It has not yet been proven by anyone but it sounds
good if you are a conspirator, to the point that you believe in
conspiracies and that sort of thing.

Well, now after this had taken place, you know there was
a large group of people running up to this area later called the
grassy knoll. Some were in uniform, and some were not. Some
had rifles. Some had pistols. And I was on the opposite side
of the street. So I got over on the other side, thinking perhaps
that they had run the assassin up into that corner. I knew it
had to be coming from the rear. So I figured they had scouted
him out and the guy was on the run, so I went across the street
to try to get a picture of the assassin right along with the rest
of the people. But my gosh, they all turned around and started
back down. It's just one of those episodes that you find when
people scatter in all directions trying to find the assassin.

I left the area, and I was joined by Jerry Haynes,[21] as I was
running back to the office. Jerry ran with me. We got green
lights at every intersection, and he was getting back to the
station because he was going to help Julie Benell[22] with her
program and he would have some information to pass on to
her at that time as well. I went on in to the *Dallas News*
building. The elevator was waiting, and I went on up to the
office. And I picked up the office telephone. Bob Johnson, our
bureau chief [Associated Press], was answering the phone,
and I told him the president had been shot. How do you know
this? I said I was taking pictures at the time, and I said Mrs.
Kennedy at the time when it occurred, she yelled out, "Oh,
no!" And then she got up and started running around,
crawling around on the back part of the deck lid of the vehicle.
This turned out to be the first eye-witness report that was

---

[21]WFAA-TV television personality who happened to be at the scene.
[22]Julie Benell had a popular food show on WFAA-TV.

circulated on our wire service. I understand we beat UPI by a minute or two. But this is something that is unavoidable when you've got two men in an automobile, one UPI, one AP, and they are fighting over the telephone and pull it right out of the connection.

Aynesworth: Ike, I'm sorry I'm going to have to stop you. They are getting the hook, and I'm going to be pulled off in a little bit. Thank you so very much, and thanks to our panel. Sorry we've run over a little bit.

FATEFUL MOMENTS:
PARKLAND, LOVE FIELD,
THE TEXAS THEATER

BERT SHIPP, Moderator

WHEN Journalists left the Texas School Book Depository area immediately after the shooting they went primarily to three separate locations—the hospital where the stricken president was being worked on by attending physicians, Love Field where Air Force One and the presidential party prepared to take off, and the Texas Theater, where an unknown individual who had just shot a Dallas police officer was captured. (This session began at 10:45 a.m. and ended at 11:45 a.m.)

Payne's introduction of Shipp. Bert Shipp, the moderator for our "Fateful Moments" panel, is well on his way toward becoming a legend in Dallas television news. Not in recent years as an on-camera personality, which is our misfortune, but as a person who has been involved in television since 1953, for 40 years now, most of that time running things from behind the scenes. Since 1975, he has been assignments editor at WFAA-TV. Before that, he was news director for 10 years. Earlier in his career, he covered every major beat in town: police, courts, city hall, education. He'll tell you about his own memorable experiences in covering the assassination, and they are memorable, as you will hear. One year after the assassination, he did what seemed to be the impossible. He got an exclusive television news interview with the Beatles during their stop over in Dallas. Maybe on another day we'll hear how that was done.

Bert has received any number of awards: AP, UPI, Press Club awards, one from SMU's Southwest Journalism Forum. He also is a past president of the Press Club of Dallas and former president of the Society of Professional Journalists. Perhaps a very recent honor is high on his personal list. He won a Press Club of Dallas Katy Award not for his television work but for writing a column. And in the same contest, his son, Brett, who works on an opposing TV station in town, KDFW, won a Katy Award for his TV reporting. It almost certainly was the first time that a father and son team won two awards in the same year. I'm proud to say that Bert attended Southern Methodist University. He's married, the father of three children and grandfather to four. Bert Shipp.

Shipp: Thank you, thank you very much. It's good to be here. I'd like to say that without Darwin and the fine people here at SMU, we would not have these digs because Jim Ewell  and Warren Bosworth and a couple of "sorries" decided sometime ago that maybe on the 30th anniversary we could get together in some dark hotel room and over serve ourselves and tell stories. Well, that was an ongoing thing for awhile, but we started picking up extra baggage. Everybody wanted to be there. First thing you know Darwin said this thing is going to be a disaster if we don't take it out on the hill [Southern Methodist University]. Thank you very much, Darwin, and all your people. We are just really indebted to you.

Shipp

I like to think many careers started at Parkland. Some ended. Parkland wasn't in existence until, well it opened in September 1954. We knew it wasn't going to be the Mayo Clinic. We knew it wasn't Bethesda Naval. It ended up more like General Hospital on TV. I had my connections with it that day back in 1963. I was at the Trade Mart. I was standing by.

A detective, he heard something on the radio. He said the president had been hit. I said, "What with? An egg? A rock? Or what?" He said he didn't know and at about that time we could hear the limousines coming down around the Trade Mart there.

Another reporter and I, Jackie Renfro,[1] we went out to the curb and shot it as it passed. We didn't see anything. Well saw Jackie, but I all I saw was a foot laying over the back of the limousine, so we jumped in a car with a detective and told him to take us to Parkland. I filmed a few scenes outside and went inside.

Inside I tried to make contact with the station. I kept pestering this one guy, and he told me he was going to show me a new trick with that phone if I didn't leave him alone. It turned out to be Merriman Smith.[2] I believe he could have. Any how, shortly thereafter I ran into Sheriff Decker[3] and I said, "What's it look like, Sheriff?" And he said, "Well, did you ever see a deer hit in the back of the head? There's nothing back there." I said, "He can't live that way."

And he says . . . and so I called the station and told John Allen [another reporter]. I said, "Tell them on the air that the president is dead. He has no way that he could live with the wound he's got in his head." And Allen said, "I won't do no such a thing." And he says, "You do it." So any how, I told them what the sheriff had told me, and I joined 2,500 others

---

[1] Of KTVT-TV, Channel 11.

[2] Smith was the United Press International White House correspondent who won the Pulitzer Prize for his instantaneous reporting that day. Riding in a pool car on loan from the telephone company, Smith managed to grab the portable radiotelephone under the dashboard because he was closest to it from his position in the middle of the front seat. "Three shots were fired at President Kennedy's motorcade today in downtown Dallas," he shouted into the telephone, then added sketchy details about the location. His brief report was reported as a bulletin by UPI at 12:34 p.m., two minutes before the presidential car reached Parkland Hospital. When Smith arrived with the motorcade at Parkland Hospital nine minutes after the shooting and saw the president's limp body, he rushed to a telephone to call UPI. The result was a "flash" indicating that the president had been "perhaps" fatally wounded.

[3] Bill Decker was the long-time sheriff of Dallas County.

who had announced the death of the president at the same time. We have a long list of every first.

We have a great panel here. Some of them are going to be connected with Parkland. Some of them are on the periphery. But they all have a great story. Bob Huffaker was a reporter with KRLD before he became Santa Claus.[4] He was one of the finest reporters around the city in those days. Bob, do you want to tell us what you saw and heard?

Huffaker: Thanks, Bert. I'm not really Santa Claus, but he is a close personal friend. It's good to see a lot of these good

Huffaker

folks. Like Jimmy Darnell, who just sat next to me. I haven't seen him for decades. And Bert as well.

We at KRLD had planned our broadcast to begin at Love Field. There Frank Glieber and Wes Wise began. Frank described the arrival of *Air Force One*, and Wes then took up the broadcast at Lemmon and Inwood. He described the motorcade at that location. And later, as you know, Wes became mayor of Dallas

and improved the image that the city had received during those days.

We were working, as some of the print media have already pointed out, with tools that are certainly primitive by today's standards. We—Frank and Wes and I—were broadcasting on little low band two-way radios. You had to hold the switch down or you were off the air. We had to depend on our KRLD tower, which still spans what is now KDFW downtown.

By the way, the way we took our cues from each other, I had a little transistor radio hanging around my neck with an ear piece in it, and that was our only means of communication as long as we were on the air. So I took my cue from Wes at Lemmon and Inwood, and then I began my broadcast from Main and Akard downtown long before the motorcade arrived. Our object was to stay on the air until Eddie Barker,

---

[4] A reference to Huffaker's long white beard.

our news director, who was to cover the matter from the Trade Mart, was to pick it up. And at that point, we were to broadcast President Kennedy's address live on both radio and television. But at this point we were just on radio. And television was broadcasting some ridiculous soap opera at the time.

I took my cue from Wes and held forth until I described the passing of the motorcade. Then I kept on, continuing with an analysis of the political reasons for Kennedy's visit to Texas as long as I could, so the motorcade would have time to reach the Trade Mart. Eddie Barker would then take over the broadcast. I was of course still broadcasting when the shots were fired in Dealey Plaza. And I was totally unaware of that, being as some of the House Select Committee[5] panelists have now told me, I was 1,500 feet away. Because they have tried desperately to pick up the shots out of my tape and have been unsuccessful in that.

Then, finally, after I held it as long as I could and assumed that Eddie must have been ready to pick it up by then, I stopped my broadcast, gave my out cue, and folded up my gear. I had KRLD's only unmarked mobile unit, a sort of a scruffy black Mercury Comet station wagon, which by the way, wherever it is, in whatever junk yard it ended up, probably bears the scars of the people who crawled all over it when the motorcade passed. I then drove the block and a half back to our KRLD newsroom, which was still in a small building outside the main building at the time, and pulled up in front, getting ready to get out of the car and go inside. Warren Fulkes, who was doing our 10 o'clock news anchor at the time, an excellent newsman, wish he were here—Warren came running out the front door and told me the president had

---

[5]The House Select Committee on Assassinations re-examined the facts surrounding the assassination in 1978, and in 1979 issued a report in which it concluded that a fourth shot had been fired at Dealey Plaza. A panel of twelve scientists appointed by the National Academy of Sciences concluded that the committee's work was "seriously flawed" and that there was no acoustical basis for the claim.

been shot and taken to Parkland Hospital. So I said, "Well, grab a camera and let's go."

It was at that point that all of us on the KRLD news team simply began to function by instinct because all of our plans for the day had gone out the window. I then made it out to Harry Hines Boulevard faster than I have ever made it anywhere else. Ran into a big cardboard box on the way out and knocked it out of the street, then got to the hospital where they had just cordoned off the entrance so that we could not get back to the emergency room through normal channels. But being a younger, much younger, newsman I simply took that old car, which was sort of new at the time, and jumped curbs all the way across the parking lot to get back to the emergency room. I had covered the emergency room and the police beat a lot as a reporter for KRLD.

Shipp: Got about a minute there, Bob.

Huffaker: That's it?

Shipp: No, you've got another minute.

Huffaker: Oh, another minute. Thanks, Bert. Thanks for the cue. I then broadcast and stayed on the air as much as possible. We stayed on the air, that was what we were trying to do, keep information coming as much as possible. And Warren Fulkes and I alternated on the microphone while the other one of us would go in meet the little press conferences given by Malcolm Kilduff[6] inside. We were giving Connally's condition and what information was being released at the time. I was interviewing [U.S. Senator] Ralph Yarborough, Congressman Ray Roberts, people like that who were still walking stunned around the back entrance of the emergency room. When Eddie finally announced that the president had died, we had not found it out even there outside the emergency room yet. I was interviewing [Congressman] Jim Wright at the

---

[6] Kilduff was the acting press secretary in the absence of Pierre Salinger, who was en route to Hawaii at the time of the assassination.

time, and it was at that point that I finally became so emotional about it that I could hardly go on. I simply said, "I know no one wants to say anything at a time like this, Congressman Wright, but do you have anything to say?" And I handed him the mike, and Jim Wright prayed into my microphone. I have always liked him ever since.

Shipp: Let's say amen to that.

Huffaker: That's right.

Shipp: Thank you, Bob.

Huffaker: And I held forth there until the hearse finally departed. Later on, my beat was the Dallas Police headquarters, where I broadcast the live CBS coverage of the shooting of Oswald, among other things, along with Nelson Benton, our associate from CBS.

Shipp: Thank you. Thank you very much. Next we have the other half of the Darnell/Welch team. Jimmy Darnell came to work for us, I worked for WBAP/KXAS in the early '60s. I knew he was going to be a great newsman because I taught him everything he knows. Jimmy, what do you remember from those days?

Darnell: Well, of course I was out at Love Field, as Bob Welch has said earlier, to get the president coming in from Fort Worth. Then I was in the motorcade. There were four of us in the Dallas bureau then for Channel 5 News. Dan Owens was on the street. I think he had come in on his day off. I'm not sure if Dan is here.

Whenever the shots were fired, I thought it was police motorcycles backfiring. I could not imagine that there had been any kind of shooting in spite of all the publicity that had been attendant to the president's visit. But I bailed out

Darnell

because my bureau chief, Jimmy Kerr, had said bail out in case there is trouble. And I thought, well OK, I don't know what that means. I don't expect anything. And so that's what I did.

I bailed out and I shot the chaos as much as I could, and our office was in the county courthouse, which is right across the street from the Texas Book Depository. My car was still at Love Field, but I did have the office, so I had unlimited access to a phone and to film, but I had no car. Also, we only had one sound camera in the entire city of Dallas for Channel 5 that I remember, and Bob Welch of course had it out at the Trade Mart for the speech. So we had to wait until a sound camera came over from Fort Worth before we could do any interviews, and by that time Henry Kokojan with NBC had joined me and we were kind of interviewing people as Jim Featherston.[7] brought them in to the press room for his own interviews, and we would take them and do the interviews, some of these people, including a Polaroid picture that someone shot.[8]

Then after we got through with that, we decided, well, I've got to get my car out at Love Field. I can't do anything else until I get my car. So Floyd Bright[9] from Fort Worth took me out to get my car. Well, we got out there and it was obvious that it was about time for the president's body to be brought back out there because of all the security and everything that was in place. So I climbed up a ladder that the police had put up to get on the roof of one of the air cargo buildings. Here looking down on Air Force One and in the foreground was this police officer who was up there standing guard. And then off to my right comes these limousines and this hearse. And I'm standing there, and they unload, they load the president's body on the plane, and I turn around, I climb down the ladder and I turn around and this deputy police chief with the Dallas Police Department says, "Let me have that. That's sacrilegious." Poor choice of words, but that's what he said. So I hand him the film, and then my bureau chief, Jimmy Kerr,

---

[7] A courthouse reporter for the *Dallas Times Herald.* See Pages 48-50.

[8] The photograph was taken by Mary Moorman.

[9] Another Channel 5 news photographer.

apparently spent a good part of the rest of the day that the president was assassinated trying to retrieve this film. To this day, it's never been seen—except there's one person who has told me that he's heard that it has been seen on the west coast or somewhere.

Shipp: Thank you. Thank you very much. Jim Ewell, the only police reporter the *Morning News* ever had. He was no Harry McCormick, I'll tell you that. Jim, can you tell us something about Parkland? Or how about Texas Theater? Give us a real good story.

Ewell: Parkland was never around that day I covered. Texas Theater was. But let me drop back just a minute to say

Ewell

what toll 30 years takes on you. I'm going to confide that last night my upper left bridge fell out. So I ask your indulgence. The fact that Tom Simmons is here is representative of the *Dallas News* editors, and Buster Haas and Bill Evans.

I still question today why they assigned a police reporter that morning, on Friday, to cover the president's arrival at Dallas Love Field. I could frankly see no sense in it because after all I was covering the police.

And that was not a matter for me to be at Love Field. I would have probably normally gone up and joined my buddies at the police headquarters for our first morning beer. But my wife doesn't know that.

But nonetheless, I did go out to Love Field, and it changed my life. Bob Welch talks about how eloquent it was, the arrival of the candidates. It was exactly that way. I left it with an extremely warm feeling from what I'd seen at Love Field. Could you ever imagine that turning down Stemmons [Freeway] that you'd meet the motorcade rushing to Parkland Hospital? I knew something was out of place because the Kennedy open limousine had one of the agents still clinging to the back deck. And I knew that was out of place.

But again they've talked about here this morning that we didn't have the technology that you've guys have got today, so I didn't know what was going on. I got to police headquarters. I had already flipped over to KLIF and heard that shots had been fired. Disbelief. I hitchhiked a ride with a former *Dallas Times Herald* reporter coming out of the building, police headquarters, now a Dallas sergeant, Jerry Hill and we made our way back down to the School Book Depository. And there I saw officers still holding their shotguns up at the windows as if they were expecting counterfire.

And then the question about the chicken bones came up. And there's another statement about that later on. And then, for some reason, the report came out on the squad car radio that a Dallas officer was down in Oak Cliff. Years later I reflected—why did I leave the biggest story ever any newsman could cover knowing that shots had been fired at a visiting president's motorcade? But for some reason, I ran and jumped in the back seat of another Dallas police car, driven by a sergeant and occupied by a captain, and we made our way in to Oak Cliff. And we made our way into the Texas Theater.

I've got to say one time I did get a chance to call my city desk from a Cabell's Minitmarket pay phone. Because I knew something was going down in Oak Cliff, somebody had shot a Dallas policeman, and I wanted a photographer because in those days spot news, reporter always tried to get their spot news photographers in line first. You could always get the story later. And I get Harvey Bogan, one of the assistant city desk editors, and he wants to know what the hell I'm doing in Oak Cliff.

I got no photographer and by that time I've got to rush back out and grab a ride in the police car, and we ended up in the Texas Theater. For some reason, I went in the balcony, and there was a scuffle down on the main floor and everything else. And I peered over the ledge, and I watched Dallas officers take that guy down. I didn't know who he was.

My esteemed colleague Kent Biffle only this morning cleared up something I've never understood as to how quickly we knew it was Lee Harvey Oswald. Once he was brought to Dallas police headquarters and the word came out he was a

Russian, defected to Russia, it changed my attitude greatly, I'll tell you. So I saw the start of the Kennedy arrival, and it ended up in the Texas Theater, and again, Oswald was taken from the Texas Theater in a car I had driven up in, had ridden up in, so again, I was hitchhiking. To this day, I don't know who I hitchhiked back in with.

Shipp: Thank you, Jim. We appreciate it. Mr. Downtown Dallas, Mr. Ron McAllister Jenkins—Jones, Smith, whatever name you are using now—were you out at Parkland?

Jenkins: Yeah, I was. I started off that day down at police headquarters. We knew right off the bat . . .

Shipp: Cut to Parkland.

Jenkins: Yeah. We knew right off the bat that something was wrong because Jim [Ewell] wasn't there. He was somewhere else. But I was at the Trade Mart with you and

Jenkins

followed what was left of the motorcade to Parkland Hospital in somewhat of a high-speed run trying to keep up and there was no possible way to do that.

By the time I got to Parkland, couldn't even get in the front drive, so I said well I know another way, so I went around the back way, through what they call the doctors' entrance at that time, and got around to the back side and came up on the emergency room from there. But as the reporters who were there will tell you, there was no way of getting in, of course, to the emergency room. That was totally sealed off by the time the bus and everyone else got there.

So I figure, well, there has got to be another way of getting in and find out what is going on. Since that was part of my beat too I finally figured out I'd go around to what they called at that time the DOA room, which of course is where they brought all the people who didn't make it for emergency treatment. It was a little late for that. And I quickly scooted around to the backside and came in the backdoor.

And the lady who ran that desk was named Fern Elliott. I'm sure a lot of reporters will remember her. And I asked her, I said, "Fern, do you know anything about what's going on?" And she said no, they are not telling me a thing. I says, "Well, I'm going to try to get around there." She says, "Well, you aren't going to get very far." And she was right. I turned a corner and there were a couple of plainclothesmen, both armed with machine guns, who said sorry, but we just can't let you pass at this point. So I said, "All right. I'll stay here then."

And I stayed in the office there, and while I was in there, this was some time later, they wheeled in a body, and I asked one of the ambulance drivers who I knew at that time, said, "Where's this coming from?" He said, "I don't know. We picked this one up over at the Texas Theater in the Oak Cliff area. It's a police officer. His name is Tippit."

And of course, I knew nothing about what was going on at the Texas Theater at that time because we were pretty much in solitary in Parkland. Well, eventually it came around and I got back outside, knowing I couldn't get anything down there, and shortly after that the word came out about the fate of the president.

And while Bert and 2,499 other reporters were the first to announce the president's death, I was the 2,501st. I never did get to because my news director had shown up by that time and he took it upon himself to take over those duties. Whereupon I found out later to my chagrin that he took my mobile unit and went his house and took a nap and I never have figured that one out. But we were there at Parkland Hospital, and of course then came the announcement that the president was dead. So we wrapped up that as much as we possibly could.

Of course, there were a lot of names being bantered around. There was the name of a Catholic priest which escapes me at present time—I think it was something like Father Huber[10]—and they said he had come out and

---

[10]The Rev. Oscar Huber.

unofficially stated that the president was dead, and a short time later, of course, we got the official word.

So there was nothing left for me to do but stay at Parkland Hospital and cover the news conference, which was by that time being announced for the governor, Governor Connally, to get his condition, and that there the only positive thing of the whole day came for me because I was right up at the front of the room there holding a microphone—I was working for KBOX radio if any of you remember the station, back during the old rock 'n' roll wars.

As I was holding the microphone and the hospital officials were giving the conditions of Governor Connally and the types of wounds, etc., I had on a watch my parents had given my from graduation from high school, and they hadn't seen me or heard from me in about a year and my mother knew I was OK because she saw my arm sticking out with the watch and the microphone. So there was some good that came out of that, but the thing I think that struck me most was what happened early that morning.

We also watched the arrival of Air Force One as it came down, and as Jim said, his life changed when he saw, I guess, the eloquence is a good word. When the plane stopped, the door opened. Nobody really came out, and then all of a sudden, President Kennedy appeared. And he had a way of doing this like no one I had ever seen before. And it was a presence bigger than life. I never knew how tall the man was, or anything else, but he looked about 7 feet tall when he came out of that door all by himself.

And then, of course, the first lady. I'll never forget that shocking pink suit she was wearing. She came up beside him. Then, of course, they broke and they went to the fence and started shaking hands. And you knew what a special person this was. A short time later, of course, it was a totally different day.

Shipp: You were there.

Jenkins: We all were.

Shipp: Thank you. If I have to tell you about Tony Zoppi we've all got problems because he was, Tony is an institution here, Las Vegas. He knew more about Dallas at night than any vampire in town. Tony had a lot of experiences and two of them occurred at Parkland that day. Tony?

Zoppi:[11] Thank you. This afternoon we are doing a panel on Jack Ruby, which is pretty much my involvement in this, and we'll leave that for this afternoon. Ruby was in my office,

Zoppi

as a matter of fact, Wednesday before the Friday. I'll tell about that this afternoon. But I went down to the Adolphus Hotel Friday morning, and Andy Anderson, the manager of the hotel, was there with Will Fritz,[12] an FBI man, good friend of ours, Breck Wall and Joe Peterson, who had a show there by the name of "Bottoms Up," and an agent for Music Corporation of America, his name was Johnny Hitt.

We were going to watch the parade, and Andy suggested, "Let's go up to the mezzanine." There's a marquee over the sidewalk, and he said we'll get a great view of the parade. So we went up there and were waiting for the parade. I don't know how many of you remember "Honest Joe," the pawnbroker, down on Elm Street. Well, we all said here comes the parade, and it was Honest Joe in his station wagon about two minutes before the parade. And everybody says, aw hell.

But eventually the parade came by and we were watching and as the presidential limousine went by, I was holding a little transistor radio, and I turned to Will Fritz [Griffith] and I said, "Will, he's so damn wide open." You know, I as a kid use to see Pathe news and they always had Secret Service men hanging all over the bumpers and on the back of the car and

---

[11]Long-time night club columnist for the *Dallas Morning News.*

[12]Zoppi later corrected himself by saying that the FBI agent was not Will Fritz, who was a homicide captain with the Dallas Police Department, but Will Griffith.

all, but this was totally wide open. I said, "Will, if this were I grenade, I could just lob it in that car." And he said, "Tony, don't even talk like that." So, they went on by, and we decided to go on in to the King's Club, which was in the Adolphus on the mezzanine, and have a bite of lunch.

And as I walked in there, Chris Elson, the owner of the club, said there's a long-distance call for you. I used to eat there every day, and if you wanted me, call the King's Club. I got on the phone, just as I started to talk, Chris came back to the office and his lips were trembling. I can see him just as plain as day. His lips were purple and trembling, and he said, "They've shot the president." I slammed down the receiver and ran back to the *News*, and Johnny King, the city editor, was more or less directing traffic. And I was a nightclub columnist, which in the journalistic profession is tantamount to a piano player in a house of ill repute. So I turned to Johnny and I said, "Listen, I'm not a front-page reporter, but I am a newspaperman. What can I do?" And Johnny said, "Aw, go out there and maybe you can take in some film from the photographers or something. Do whatever you can." But at least I had an assignment.

So I got back in my car, and I got there about quarter of a mile from the hospital, cars parked all over the place. I pull into an empty space and ran over to the hospital, and I was at the emergency dock.

And the first thing I saw was the limousine with the roses in the back seat. I got up on the emergency dock and started walking to the emergency entrance, and two Secret Service men said, "Where are you going?" I said, "I'm going to the hospital." They said, "Who are you?" I said, "I'm Tony Zoppi of the *Dallas News*." "Let me see your press pass." Well, I never carried a press pass because, well, I felt like I didn't need one. I had a daily column and a TV show and I knew everybody around town. They wouldn't let me in, and I was the most frustrated newspaperman in the world. Standing out there on that dock, knowing that everybody else was in the hospital. And about that time an O'Neal ambulance pulled up to the dock and backed in, and the driver and his helper got out and opened the back door and I saw this huge bronze casket. Up until then nobody knew for sure whether he was dead or alive. There were rumors that Connally had been killed or was not, and that the president was hurt and he wasn't hurt. When I saw that casket I said he's dead. And they were trying to lift that casket onto a gurney and they couldn't lift it, it was so heavy, so the driver turned to me and said, "Grab a corner, will you?" And I grabbed a corner of the casket and the fellow next to me grabbed a corner and we lifted it onto the gurney. And I started to let go but the Secret Service men, the ones that wouldn't let me in, they are saying, "Come on, come on." So I just held on and I followed. Boy, I am going to get in. And I did something that to this day, I can't explain. As we're rolling that casket into the hospital, I reached underneath it, and I put my fingerprints as hard as I could on the bottom of that casket. I'm still trying to explain why I did it, other than the fact that I figured, well, he's going to be in this casket and I want him to know that Tony Zoppi helped carry the casket in, if nothing else. I think that's the closest I can come to explaining it.

But I got in the hospital. Now they said follow the yellow line, which we did, right down to the trauma room. Now I could really see the story of the century. We got right up to the door, and a little Secret Service fellow, about 5-foot-8, I can see him just as plain as day, he says, "We'll take it from here, gentlemen." And I say, "Oh, No, we got . . . " And he says, "We'll take it from here." And I say don't press your luck.

And I looked over, and there's a bank of phones on the opposite wall. So I went over to one of the phones, and a man answered. And I gave him the number of the *Dallas News*. I said, "Get me the *Dallas News*." And the man says, "Get the hell off this line." The line went dead. The FBI, I learned later, had tied up all the phones.

But there was a stairwell, and down at the bottom of the stairs I noticed this girl at a switchboard, the old-time, plug-in switchboard. So I ran down there and said, "I'm Tony Zoppi with the *Morning News*." And she says, "Yeah, I read your column every morning." I said, "Do me a favor. Get me a phone and get me the *Dallas News*." She said, "Go in that office and use that black phone on the desk."

So I went in there. She put the call through, and Johnny King, who had sent me out there rather reluctantly, he answered the phone. I said, "Johnny. This is Tony Zoppi. The president is dead." Which made me the 2,502nd.

So he says, "How the hell do you know?" Because he had all his top people out there. And I said, "I just carried in his casket." And Johnny says, "You sure?" And I said, "I'm positive. Johnny, he's dead." He says, "You better be right." And I said, "I'm right." Because they were figuring about putting out an extra. And they had to make damn sure because nobody in the *News* at that time had heard the confirmation. And I don't want to run over my time because I have a lot of Jack Ruby stories.

Shipp: That story is to be continued.

Zoppi: Right.

Shipp: Thank you, Tony. Hugh Aynesworth has already been introduced. His fabulous background has been relayed to you. I talked Hugh into adding maybe a few "P.S.es" to what we have going here this morning.

Aynesworth: Thank you Bert. I won't take much time because my panel ran over so long we are in trouble here. But I mentioned after we left the Depository building we heard about an officer being shot and I ran over there to interview people. Got with two Channel 8 people—Vic Robertson and I can't remember the other one, and we drove like mad men to get over there, interviewed all those people.

And from there there was a tip who was the suspect, whoever it was, was in a furniture store, an old furniture store over on Jefferson.

And I've been asked a lot of times was I ever scared. I was not scared when the shooting went off because there were so many people I guess I felt the odds against them getting me might be, you know, several hundred to one. But the only time I was scared, I went into that furniture store, and there were six or seven or eight cops, whatever, some plain clothes, a couple in uniform, and all of a sudden—we're going through and it is just stacked up, it's dusty, it's dirty, it's not a place of business, it's a storage furniture place—and all of a sudden somebody comes piling through the second floor, up to here, his feet coming down. And I thought, "Oh God, that's him, whoever he is. That's the guy who killed the cop." And I looked around and everywhere I saw everyone had a gun except me. And at that point I was scared.

Pretty soon we got out of there. There was nothing except cops looking after other cops. Soon we got a report about the Texas Theater, that a suspect entered there and all cars in the vicinity should go there. That was only four or five blocks, so I ran like the devil and got in there just about, I would assume less than a minute before Oswald was captured.

I remember looking through the thing and already the lights had been brought up a little bit. There was about half lights on, and there were people coming up both aisles. And I noticed one time they stopped somebody else, I guess to throw Oswald off. They knew where he was because the man who had pointed the finger at him which resulted in the police being called was Johnny Brewer, who had a shoe store four doors down.[13] And he had seen Oswald cringe and sort of off to one side when the cars with sirens went by and after they went by he followed Oswald out to the thing and he thought it was unusual and saw him go into the theater. He was the one who later went in the back and told the police, "That's him there."

But they didn't want to go straight to Oswald because they didn't know if he was armed or not. Then they jumped him. There were six or seven total, I guess. I have talked with probably five of them. I think there were two others who I did not talk to.

Oswald made quite a fight for a little guy. I remember he was yelling, "I protest this police brutality." He said that three or four times.

One thing I never understood. There was a policeman, as they brought him out, there was a policeman with a big Stetson. He kept holding it over his face so that some of the

[13]Brewer was manager of Hardy's Shoe Store.

photographers didn't get his face for awhile. I never understood why he was protecting him that way.

Afterward, I don't know where I got this, I asked Jim Ewell if he told me, but later that afternoon I started going around to the places where Oswald lived. I don't know where I got those addresses, I really don't. But I remember one time it was very embarrassing. I went to one of the places where Oswald lived, I believe on Neely Street, and I knocked and I knocked and I knocked because I wanted to find out if anyone knew him. This man who was in sort a stage of undress came to the door, very angry at me, and spoke Spanish and did not speak much English. He could not understand why I was there and I could not understand what he was doing and I looked and I saw he had a lady friend that he was doing it with and I got out of there in a hurry.

Earlier—I'll make this very brief—I went by 1026 [North] Beckley and interviewed the lady who was the landlady there at great length.[14] And one thing—she tried to give me the signature thing that Oswald had signed in, O.H. Lee, and she said the FBI just left and they didn't take this so do you want this, you want this? And I said no, I don't want this. They will be back for it, I bet. But that's about the extent of that day for me.

Shipp: Thank you very much, Hugh. Thank all of you. Appreciate you letting me hold you feet to the fire because these guys have great stories and all of them could have gone on all day long. Thank you very much for your patience and you attendance here.

---

[14]Earlene Roberts was the landlady at Oswald's rooming house, 1026 N. Beckley.

THE SEARCH FOR DETAILS: THE POLICE STATION

JIM EWELL, Moderator

When the accused assassin was arrested in the Texas Theater after having allegedly shot and killed a Dallas police officer, he was brought to the jail at the Dallas Police Station. The press congregated in large numbers on the building's third floor, seeking details of evidence accumulated and of the interrogation of the suspect, Lee Harvey Oswald. (This session began at 1:15 p.m. and ended at 2:15 p.m.

Payne: After Oswald's arrest there was great pressure from the growing numbers of journalists who congregated at the Dallas police department, stationing themselves on the third floor where the homicide offices were located. What evidence did the police have on Oswald?

The police reporter for the *Dallas Morning News* was Jim Ewell, who will moderate the "Search for Details" panel. It is quite likely that no other Dallas journalist covered police longer than Jim. He was there on the beat for more than twenty-five years. I recall story-after-story bearing Jim's by-line, and as the weekend and substitute police reporter for the *Times Herald* for a few of those years, it often fell my lot to have to follow a Ewell story. And with his sources at the police department, that was a tough thing to do. Jim was born and reared in West Central Texas. He started his newspaper career as an unpaid reporter for the *Cisco Daily Press* while he was still in high school. He graduated to the *Abilene Reporter-News* in 1949, and worked as a stringer for the Fort Worth and Dallas papers. When he moved to Dallas in 1953 he went to work for the *Times Herald,* but two years later he switched to the *Morning News.* In 1981 Jim was hired by Dallas County Sheriff Don Byrd to supervise his media relations, and there Jim has stayed. He now supervises media relations for Sheriff Jim Bowles. He and his wife Ruby have one son and three daughters; two sons-in-law, and three grandchildren. Jim and his wife live in DeSoto. Jim Ewell.

Ewell: We're going to depart just for a minute here to accommodate one of our panelists who has to catch a plane back to San Antonio. In the beginning when Darwin sent out the forms for us in the old media then to fill back in and send and give us a thumbnail sketch of what we did that day. Now, Tinsley, for instance is a newspaperman, so he gave us a thumbnail sketch of himself right here covering some 31 years at the *Fort Worth Star-Telegram.* The other reporters did the same. Associated Press photographers did the same. But then we come to a radio man, we come to a radio man, and this gives the whole story—page after page. (laughter) At the time he was a reporter for KLIF, the old KLIF, and now he is in San Antonio, still active as a result of this right here, and I'd like to introduce now as our first panelist who has to rush from here to catch a flight back, Gary DeLaune.

DeLaune: Thank you, Jim, and I apologize, but the strike[1] as you well know set everything back. They said if you want to stay on standby be ready by 8 o'clock. I said OK, so we have an earlier flight.

There were four guys in those days who I counted on as sources as the police department. One was Sergeant Jerry Hensley, two was Walter Potts of the homicide division. He was my confidante in homicide. And three was George Carter

---

[1] A reference to the strike by flight attendants at American Airlines.

of the *Times Herald,* and the fourth was Jim Ewell. And they felt sorry for the guy who was the lone police reporter for KLIF. "The Old Scotchman,"[2] you know, he was named appropriately all right.

The police reporter for KLIF News and as you well know even in those days with top 40 there was a lot of pressure to

DeLaune

continuously report the news when it happened, and Jack Ruby was a hanger-on, he was a groupie. Tony Zoppi is going to tell you a lot more about Jack. He knew him far better than most people in Dallas. Jack Ruby was a kind of nuisance guy, a little harmless creature. He hung around KLIF. He had a great friend there in Russ Knight, the "Weird Beard."[3] He would hang around KLIF and they'd bowl every night at the Cotton Bowling Palace at Inwood and Lemmon Avenue. And Jack for some reason he thought we were his heroes. And he would bring us by Carousel Club passes and ask us to come to the club and everything, and so the day of the assassination after I had reported the national story and all of our people got back into the studio, Gordon McLendon sent me to the Trade Mart but I didn't get to go there because of the shooting. So he said you know all the policemen, you know all the contacts, so you go over to the police department.

So, all afternoon into the night, even after the arrest of Oswald and the shooting of Tippit, I was there for many, many hours, hadn't had a break for coffee or anything and I was stuck in the press room. We were feeding out reports every ten or fifteen minutes. So Jack had been coming to the KLIF studios. He immediately got in his car and rushed to the KLIF studios. He still had his two poodles in the car, and in the back seat was a stack of pamphlets on H.L. Hunt's

---

[2]Gordon McLendon, the owner and top radio personality for KLIF, nicknamed himself "The Old Scotchman" (eschewing the correct term, "Scotsman") for his recreated broadcasts of major league baseball games.

[3]A popular disk jockey at KLIF.

"Lifeline,"[4] if you remember that old radio show. But Jack was a big listener to that show, the H.L. Hunt show.

So, anyway, he just bothered everybody to death and people—secretaries—were thrown into reporting news, and the phone lines were just jammed. And so finally, to get rid of Jack, they said, "Jack, Gary DeLaune has been there at the police department for eight or ten hours. He hasn't had any break. Can you take him some sandwiches?" And so Jack said, "Yeah, yeah."

So he goes somewhere and buys a sackful of sandwiches and parks his car in the lot, and a lot was made of this later when they said Jack Ruby's car was found in the parking lot with two thousand and eight dollars in it. Well, Jack always had a lot of money as Tony I'm sure will tell you, and he always carried a .38. But anyway, he came to the police department, and not being familiar with where the press room was—it was on the third floor in those days and when you went into the police department you went down the stairs into the police locker room area, and over to the right was a room—oh, 20 x 35 or so as the line-up room. So Jack, instead of going up the stairs into the elevator to the third floor just inadvertently went down the steps and saw all this confusion, and I think someone mentioned earlier—I don't know if it was you [Ewell] or who—but they said about the lack of security. That's true, there was no security around the police department. And, uh, you could just wander through and so Jack instead of coming up to the third floor and bringing me the sandwiches went into the line-up room.

And later Eva Grant, his rather eccentric sister, more or less theorized that Jack let it spawn in his mind to become the avenging angel. He wanted to be somebody. He had grown up on the west side of Chicago, as Tony will elaborate later. But he wanted to be somebody and this was his chance. So this spawned in his mind—instead of bringing the sandwiches then for a day and a night, it spawned in his brain to do something.

So that morning, and there was another in the JFK movie,

---

[4] A radio show sponsored by Hunt to espouse his right-wing political views.

for instance, a lot was made about somebody opening the door and Jack walking through, which was hogwash. Jack simply walked down the ramp. I know because I walked down the ramp and there was no security. All the policemen— everybody, secret service, there was a half-moon-shaped a cordon of press and police officers, and I was looking almost across the room at Ike Pappas and Tom Pettit. I was directly across from them. And I was standing right next to Bob Jackson and Jack Beers, and Bob just remembered last night that, that's right, that I was standing next to him, and if I could just have a piece of that photography, I'd have been all right.

But that morning after Jack had spawned this a couple of days, that morning our news director had said, "Gary, you've been up so long. We're not going to cover that. It's going to be an early-morning transfer. We don't need to cover the transfer of Oswald." Well, I told my wife, it was about 5:30 when I woke up, I said, "I've got to go. I know, I've just got a feeling. I've got to be down there." So I dressed and went to the police station, and this was the story I got from Chief Curry. I don't know if this was confirmed or elaborated with you [Jim Ewell] or Bob [Jackson] or Wes [Wise], but Jesse told me that he relented to the network demand to transfer Oswald at 9:30[5] rather than 4:30 a.m. which was the initial time set to transfer him. And he bowed to network pressure so they could have the pool camera televise Oswald. So, Ruby, as I walked down the ramp, I know Ruby had got in that way because there was only one police officer directing traffic, and he was looking the other way. So I just walked in and saw these guys standing there, and about that time is when it happened, and the rest is history. You know what happened, and with the

---

[5]Curry had been under intense pressure from all journalists on Saturday evening at the police station to tell them when Oswald would be transferred from the temporary jail facility at the police station to the more permanent county jail. They were seeking an opportunity to rest after their lengthy vigilance at the police station, and they stressed to Curry that they needed to be present to see the transfer. Curry promised the persistent journalists that nothing of substance would happen before 10 a.m. the next morning, an implied commitment that he would not transfer Oswald earlier than that.

results and repercussions, but it didn't come out later. It was in the *New York Times* on a Monday morning. It said that Jack Ruby had initially gone to the police department looking for a Joe "Delong." Well, Joe Long was our news director, and they got me confused with him, and then during the appeals case Phil Burleson called me to testify one day and as I was sworn in Jack yelled at me across the room. He said, "Gary, I was looking for you, where were you?" And I said, "Jack, you just couldn't find me; I was there." So that's how it all came about that Jack Ruby came to the police station looking for me when he first got the idea to become the avenging angel for Jackie Kennedy. And it was a great thrill for me to be a part of history, not so much that I got to cover it but because I got to stand next to the guy that got to shoot it. Thank you.

Ewell: Picking up from where Gary left off to get back on the focus of this panel, that morning the young president had been murdered, a Dallas officer had been shot down on an Oak Cliff street, and then the police arrest a suspect. Prior to that time, all the focus for those who had been flying in—the national media and everybody else—was at Parkland Hospital, back at the downtown scene and everything else, and then suddenly they had a suspect. He is now downtown at the Dallas police headquarters. The focus turned there, very very quickly. I can remember now that to all of us who had been up there to maintain a lifetime up there, we knew police headquarters simply as 210 South Harwood. And for the first time, in my opinion, since the Civil War a major government building was captured by the media. Picking up from there, I'd like next to introduce Jack Tinsley, of the *Fort Worth Star-Telegram.* Tinsley is one of those persons that we at the *Dallas News* and the *Dallas Times Herald*, we heard his name but I never got to meet him. I met him for the first time today. He has been with the *Fort Worth Star-Telegram* for now about thirty-one years. Is still active on that newspaper—very, very well known newspaperman in Texas. Jack can come forward now and pick up where it was in the maelstrom of confusion. It was as if the building had been turned upside down. I could not believe that my old haunts up there had now been captured by outside reporters from the *New York Times, Chicago Tribune,* the Nipponese, the French, the Germans, and everybody else were pouring in by Friday night. Jack, what was the kind of scene you found?

Tinsley: Well, like so many others who have been up here today, I'd like to back up a few minutes first. Your mention of the lengthy bio that Gary had and how some of the panelists have run overtime this morning because in print journalism, and I'm sure broadcast, too, how important brevity is. They're always saying keep the story short, keep it brief, reminds me

Tinsley

of the story in the old days of the young cub reporter who went to work and was assigned to write a story about a man who had expired in an elevator accident. And he went out and covered the story and wrote his heart out and wrote a lengthy story and turned it into the old city editor, the kind that used to bark at you, and the guy just threw it back to him and said, "Shorten it." So he went back and dutifully shortened it, and then he came back with

the next version and the guy said, "Too long, shorten it." By this time the young cub was getting very frustrated, so he went to his typewriter and returned in a matter of seconds, and the story read: "Jay Smith looked up an elevator shaft to see if the elevator was on its way down. It was. Age 59."

I don't know if we can be that short, but I would like to say—earlier this morning they had mentioned the panel about what some of the newspapers did, and we're very proud that the *Star-Telegram* also did two extra editions. Both of them, the front pages are over here against the wall. We did an extra on Friday afternoon after we had completed the complete run of the evening edition of the *Star-Telegram*. There were eight major replatings, or chasers that afternoon, and then we turned around and did 30,000 extra copies and sold those on the street corners, and then Sunday afternoon after the Oswald shooting, we put together an extra edition and sold another 30,000 on the street corners of Fort Worth and Dallas, as fast as we could get them out we sold the papers. So we're very proud of that.

Also, I'd like to mention that on those pages over there on the Friday morning there is a page that has a large reverse headline over the skyline of a darkened Fort Worth that says "Welcome, Mr. President." That was done by the late Lorn McMullen, and we're very proud of that because that was the same day that Kennedy started his day, and there was that scurrilous ad in an unnamed Dallas newspaper. But we are very proud of what we did that weekend and some of you may not know that the Texas Associated Press Managing Editors Association awarded first place for spot news coverage in 1964 to the *Fort Worth Star-Telegram*, the *Houston Chronicle*, and the *Dallas Times Herald*. It was a shared arrangement.

I would like to say that I was in the Hotel Texas the night Kennedy arrived, and not 2 a.m. as I recall but about 11:30 p.m. the hotel lobby was jammed. The scene was electric. I don't know how many of you really remember what kind of role model the Kennedys were, but it was a different era—the glamour, I mean. There was an awful lot of hope in America, particularly among the young people coming off of eight years of General Eisenhower, who was a trusted grandfather, but this was a whole new arrangement. So there was electricity in the air. I was there as they came in, and the next morning he was going to speak at the Fort Worth Chamber of Commerce breakfast at 8 a.m., which was sold out, 800 people, but 2,000 working people gathered in the parking lot across from the hotel in a light mist of rain. And the president came out and addressed those people, and he said that Mrs. Kennedy would normally be here but she was getting ready, but then when she does get ready she looks a lot better than we do, which drew a chuckle from the crowd. Anyhow, he did that and went on back in and I followed the motorcade back to Carswell Air Force Base and drove back to the office.

By the time I got to the office there were reports of shots being fired, so "Chief" [Horace] Craig and all the other editors emptied all of us out and said, "Go to Dallas." And I was in a car with the late Elston Brooks, with Mike Cochran, and Tony Record, a photographer.And we sped to Parkland Hospital. And as we went in there, the thing that I was really impressed by was that in hitting Harry Hines [Boulevard]—it has an esplanade—there were no cars on the road. Cars were parked on the esplanade and on each side it was kind of an eerie scene. And so we went to the hospital, and of course we couldn't get in there, but I looked down the hallway and I saw a casket being wheeled in. At the time I didn't know anything. I didn't know whose it was. It may have been Kennedy's, or it may have been Tippit's, I'm not sure.

At any rate, we saw that we weren't going to get anything there, so I hitchhiked downtown to the School Book Depository. I don't know what time this was, but it was early because the School Book Depository had not been sealed off[6] and I got the foreman to take me up to the sixth floor and show me the window and the brown bag and all of that. And I was writing notes and putting everything down, and then I was looking for a telephone but I couldn't find one there, so I went across the street to this four-story building over there.[7] I don't even know what the name of it was, but I got on the elevator and it went to the fourth floor. And I got the telephone. I called in because as I said we were "chasing"[8] all afternoon.

---

[6]Initially, the School Book Depository had been sealed off, as Tom Alyea and Kent Biffle describe in their statements on pages 36-41 and 50-52. But after some two hours had passed officers permitted the handful of newsmen remaining at the scene [by now, most of the journalists were at Parkland Hospital or at the Dallas Police Station] to come into the building. They were able to go to the sixth floor, see where the rifle had been found, observe the corner where boxes of books had been placed to conceal the sniper's nest, and peer out the sixth floor window from where shots had been fired.

[7] The building, actually seven stories high, has had several names over the years. When first built in 1902 it was known as the Kingman-Texas Implement Co. building. Later it became known as 501 Elm Place.

[8]"Chasing" is a newspaper term for replating a page, usually page one, as a news story changes and placing it on the press as soon as ready without regard to edition changes.

And when I got through calling in I started talking to employees up there. There were little old ladies—it was a dress factory, and they were telling me about their boss who had taken a video of the motorcade. And so it sounded interesting, and I took down notes and did enough for a little six-inch sidebar that appeared on the back page of the first section of the next morning's *Star-Telegram*. And of course the man turned out to be Abraham Zapruder.

And then later I went down to the Dallas police station. I don't know what time it was, but it was probably sometime between 4 and 6 p.m. And as I recall there only three of us in the press room down there.

And pretty soon Oswald was brought in at the far right end, and he was with a detective. I noticed his face was puffed up because they had laid it on him pretty good when they had captured him I guess at the Texas Theater. And one of the reporters there—I don't know who it was—but he lost control and he saw Oswald down there and he reached up with his fist and said, "You killed the President." And they ducked Oswald off into a room.

Obviously they were in the process of questioning him, and there was other thing I would like to mention. It was very hard to get a telephone that day, you may remember, and Jerry Flemmons was able to go down into the basement of the—he was one of our reporters[9]—into the basement of Parkland, where they had a lab down there, and he got the lab assistant to keep a line open to the *Star-Telegram*, so our reporters fed information through him down at the basement so we were able to get our story in.

Ewell: Thank you, Jack. You remember, too, that as the swarm of reporters began gathering that Friday night at word of Oswald's arrest and everything, there was already a strong inference by authorities including District Attorney Henry Wade and everything else that they had now a suspect in the shooting of the president in addition to the police officer. And

---

[9] *Fort Worth Star-Telegram.*

how suddenly like you say telephones became a very premium thing.

Taking it up from there is Ferd Kaufman, then a photographer for the Associated Press, well-known to all newsmen around the Dallas-Fort Worth area who had to deal with Ferd. But yet he was one of those who was an involved photographer. I am told now that I can introduce Ferd Kaufman of the Associated Press, so pick it up now, Ferd, tell us what you found around Captain Will Fritz' office.

Kaufman: In a word: pandemonium. I had been like a lot of people assigned to go to Fort Worth to the breakfast meeting, which I did, and then I was supposed to arrive at the Trade Center, which of course I did, and it became evident very quickly that something was amiss.

So I left there and went back to the AP office. A phone rang, and I don't know who the call was from, but they said that they had caught an individual at the Texas Theater. So Harold Waters, who was there in the office with me, we

Kaufman

jumped in my car and headed over Zangs [Boulevard] and got probably to—I don't even remember the name of the street—but we saw this police car coming back with a driver and two officers and another individual in the back seat. So playing the hunch, we turned around and beat them back to the police station. And they really weren't running very fast. I bailed out of the car somewhere in the middle of Commerce Street and went in, and they brought this individual in and I made a picture, and my slight claim to fame was it was the first picture of the guy [Oswald] in captivity.

The rest of the time I just lived in the hallway. Every hour that passed, more people arrived, and it became just a madhouse. And you all know that "Hail Mary" is what Roger Staubach did to the end zone. Well, in our world "Hail Mary" was trying to get a picture above the heads of everybody. And if you remember what Bill Winfrey showed—that picture today, which happens to be one of the great pictures—I am in that picture cocking my camera because they had just brought him past me. And so I just spent the rest of the weekend there.

And I managed to miss the action.[10] The AP had decided that on the transfer of Oswald to the county that I would go down there with the UPI photographer, Pete Fisher, and be the pool when he got there. So we were down there at the [county] jail with our noses pressed against the bars waiting for the transfer, and they had live television down there.

And of course we saw the shooting, and again drove back to the police station. I don't know, Harold [Waters], where we left the car that time. But that was basically my part in that I spent the weekend there, and I have thought in later years as every hour passed more and more people arrived and this hallway just became an absolute disaster area. I mean it was just swamped and the few weeks after that I was thinking about it, and I thought, "Boy, if some nut had gone in there and dropped a hand grenade we would all have been dead." And that's my story.

Ewell: Charmayne Marsh was to be a member of this panel, and I'm really sorry that she is not here because she is another one that was caught in the American Airlines strike, now working in Washington, D.C., but just to say a little bit about the reporters coming in from all corners of the world to cover the story in Dallas.

Charmayne Marsh at that time was a journalism student at the University of Texas at Austin, and she would tell you the story of how she and other reporters—student reporters—from the *Daily Texan*[11] got to Dallas to cover the story, too. And maybe if we have time we might get back in there because some of the members of the journalism staff from the University of Texas are here, and if we get a chance maybe Darwin can work them in later on. But now, I'd like to continue with Darwin Payne now, who, being our coordinator

---

[10] A reference to the shooting of Oswald on Sunday by Jack Ruby.

[11] The student newspaper at the University of Texas.

for this event today, now turns back to being a reporter thirty years ago and at the Dallas police headquarters, 210 South Harwood.

Payne: OK, thanks, Jim. Yes, on Saturday afternoon it was my regular duty to go to the police station and work weekend police. So, of course, that Saturday was a very eventful time and I anticipated it greatly. When I showed up at city hall I remember these huge trucks out on the street with their cables going up to the third floor windows for the live telecasts from there. I expected that I might have difficulty getting onto the third floor, where the press room was and the homicide offices, and I don't think that I had a press pass either. I know Tony [Zoppi] mentioned that before, but everybody did not carry a press pass then.

So I caught the elevator, went up to the third floor and was very surprised that nobody said a word to me. I just walked on in and joined the crowd. And what a mob scene it was. I agree totally with the others. It was incredible the number of people there, the action there, and I recall there were people who had no connection whatsoever with the press there. In particular there was one teen-ager wearing a sailor suit. Why in the world he was there on the third floor I didn't know, but I asked him and he said well, yes, he was in the Navy, but he was doing a story for his high school paper.

And, uh, there was another reporter there, Jim Koethe,[12] who was with the *Times Herald,* and we were working together for a while, and as Captain Fritz or the police chief would come out with an announcement ever so often or they would bring Oswald through the halls the press would run to that scene and listen to the press conference. So we worked out an arrangement whereas we took turns. When they had a mini-press conference one of us would cover that. The other would go to the press room down at the end of the hall and grab a telephone so we would have a line. That was a great problem for the reporters. As I recall there were two, perhaps three

---

[12]Koethe later was murdered under mysterious circumstances, an event which proved gist for many conspiracy theorists.

telephones in that press room. Jim [Ewell] will remember for sure; so we worked out that system that worked pretty well.

I remember, too, Chief Curry in particular at one of those press conferences, all the reporters, photographers, crowding around him, squeezing around him, and one reporter having the nerve—I thought it was nervy—of putting his notepad on Chief Curry's back and taking notes on his back, using it as a pad. Rather surprising, to me. I recall also the print journalists such as myself began to get a little bit irritated at all the television persons who were there, the network TV people, because every time an official would come out the lights would go on, they would start the press conference, and it would be the television people who were getting all the information. We were shut out from the offices, the print people were, so we just, as I recall, stood there taking notes that the television people were dominating. They were dominating the interviews, and this of course has been seen as a transitional period in journalism when television began to be more dominant, and I recall distinctly being a little put off by that.

There was great pressure on Chief Curry by the press to let them know when he was going to transfer Oswald the next day. Because many of these reporters had been here since the day before, Friday afternoon. They had come in as quickly as they could. I'm sure they spent most of Friday night up and they were desperate for sleep; they were tired, and you could see that in their disheveled appearances.

And so Chief Curry finally agreed that if they came back the next day—as I recall 10 o'clock—if they waited until 10 o'clock to come they would miss nothing. Which was to say that he would transfer Oswald after 10 on Sunday morning. So that announcement came maybe at 10 o'clock, 10:30 in the evening on Saturday, and after he assured the newsmen of that, they took off and left. I mean all of them. There may have been one or two, but I was there because I normally stayed there until about 1 a.m., and the *Dallas Morning News* reporter was there. That was Johnny Rutledge, who was a police reporter for a long time, too. And the two of us were there alone as I recall it in the press room for maybe two hours or so until I went home at about 2 a.m. And at about 12 o'clock, as I recall, I got a telephone call from our city desk in the press room telling me that there was—and I think this was Charlie Dameron, I talked to Charlie about it—he was on the panel this morning and I think he was called to the telephone to elaborate on this message. Someone else had given me the original information.

But there was a report that Dan Rather had had a story on WCBS Radio I think it was saying that the Dallas Police Department had in custody an eyewitness who could identify Oswald as the one pulling the trigger, firing the shots. What did I know about that? The story was rather vague. It was just a report about a radio story.

Well, I didn't know anything about that. I had no idea that they might have someone in protective custody or in custody, but it was my assignment to find out. There was Rutledge sitting quietly at the other desk in the press room and I could imagine—I supposed it was possible the *Dallas Morning News* has this story wrapped up, and it's going to be their banner story the next morning. And, you know, here I am, only been at the *Times Herald* about three months at that time. I've got to get the story. So I talked to the night police chief—I think it was [Jack] Tanner, I can't remember for certain. No, he knew nothing about it. You know, it was possible, but certainly he knew nothing about it. And so, looked around some more, couldn't find anything, called back to the office, and was desperate. I had no details about it.

Finally, we concluded, and this would have been about 12:30, perhaps even 1 a.m., just before our final edition. So we concluded that I would call Chief Curry at home. I hated to do that. I knew the chief had been under such pressure all this time; you can't imagine such pressure, and at 1 a.m. or 1:30— somewhere around that time—obviously I was going to wake him up if I called him. But we had the telephone number.

I called him at home and his wife answered the phone, obviously sound asleep. You how you can always tell. "Yes," she said, "I'll give you the chief." And he was obviously in bed next to her, and in just a second he took the telephone, also sound asleep and I tried to explain to him the information that I had. I was trying to confirm it. Was this true or not?

I couldn't make the chief understand what I was saying. It was as if—I don't mean this in a disparaging way whatsoever—he must have taken sleeping pills so that he could go to sleep that night. And it was as if he were in a dream. You know how someone talks as if they are in a dream. You can't make sense out of their comments. I went on and on, desperately trying to make him understand. I scribbled down notes thinking perhaps later on I could make sense out of these notes, which I couldn't, and so I finally gave up—let him go, and reported back to the paper there was nothing.

Well, as it turned out there was no such person. I don't know about the source of that story. It's possible that there may have been such a story referring to Howard Brennan[13]— you saw him on the videotape this morning—because I think he was assured by police that he would be watched over, or something like that.

But another key point to this story. Later on I read in the Warren Commission Report—not the single volume—I think somewhere in the twenty-six volumes that there was an assassination threat made anonymously to the FBI later that night. And Sheriff Bill Decker was informed of it. Sheriff Decker attempted to call Chief Curry in the middle of the night to tell him about this assassination threat, and his purpose was to say, "Chief we've got to transfer him tonight. We can't wait until tomorrow because of this threat. Let's do it while the press is gone, while the people are gone." And the report was that the telephone was out of order, that the line was constantly busy, and it's quite obvious to me that the chief had taken his telephone off the hook after I called him. And so, Decker couldn't reach him. So, end of my story.

---

[13]Brennan was viewing the presidential motorcade from a vantage directly across the street from the Texas School Book Depository. He told reporters and the Warren Commission that he had seen a man whose description resembled closely that of Oswald firing the shots at President Kennedy from the sixth-floor window.

Ewell: Thank you, Darwin. You opened up two comments. In those days in 1963 and that period, public officials did not have unlisted phone numbers at their residence.[14] You could call them at home. Just shortly before he retired we were walking in the police basement and Curry said, "Why is it, Jim, all you reporters wait until after I go home to call me?" I said, "Chief, trust me. When you're no longer chief of police in Dallas, Texas, you won't be getting any phone calls."

And that was so true, because later on Jesse Curry went on to become a director of security for one of the downtown businesses. And we met at Titche's.[15] and he brought it up. He said, "Ewell, I want to tell you something. Nobody calls me any more." In that period between the shooting of the president and the police officer and the arrest and then the shooting of Lee Harvey Oswald by Jack Ruby, what set up after that was an intense competition. Considering this, we had the best of the best from the outside press. We met them. And here we were, Dallas, Texas, reporters, radio, newspaper, television, and everything else, and we were now competing on a world-wide story against these guys. And don't you think, Darwin, and you guys around will remember this and everything else, that we had to do a lot more work. We had to keep our feet to the pedal because we did not want to be outdone by an outside reporter. How embarrassing.

And so I think that in itself—by the time Oswald was in custody and had been identified and the district attorney was coming down to state to the world and everything else that they were going to file charges that he killed the president and also Officer Tippit. The press had already got four of the five W's—who, what, when, and where. And now, you guys, don't you think—the big drive among us all that time was to answer the why. That was what everybody was struggling against, Darwin and Jack, all you print guys, television and everything else. We wanted to know the answer to why. Why Kennedy? Why Tippitt? Why Oswald?

---

[14]Curry's number, however, was unlisted.

[15]A major department store in Dallas, Titche-Goettinger, no longer in business.

Now it's up to debate whether or not we've ever answered why. Whether or not the Warren Commission ever answered why. And that remains as—like Eddie Barker said the other day and everything else. There is not a day goes by that somebody doesn't bring up the Kennedy assassination for discussion. And everyone else in this room can relate to that. We've got a little extra time. Can I ask a question?

Payne: I'd like to ask about that boy in a sailor suit. Was there anybody else who saw that boy in a sailor suit on that Saturday night. Or what you saw even? [An anonymous voice from the assembled newsmen recalls having seen the sailor.] You remember him, right?

Ewell: Do you remember, too, that Ferd Kaufman alluded to this, and Jack I'll bet you remember this, too—by Friday night or especially Saturday morning when everybody in the media had marshaled all their forces down there. It was so jammed up and everything you couldn't maneuver. I mean, like Ferd was talking about, he couldn't even click his camera. There were people who were trying to take notes with part of their pen wedged up in their nose nostrils, you know, because it was that   tight—tight space. The local reporters were blocked out from their own telephones, their own desks. We had some sympathetic Dallas detectives in one office that allowed us behind locked doors to come in and use the telephones. The day that Hugh Aynesworth and I, that Sunday afternoon, were feeding in reports back to the *News* on the shooting of Oswald, we were dictating from one of those phones in Burglary and Theft while the rest of the gang was outside blocked out and we knew that if we controlled the telephone we could control our story.

I'll never forget, and you guys remember it, too, that television recorded this one little reporter, every time that Captain Will Fritz would show up—incidentally they couldn't even get out of their offices to go back out on the street to expand the investigation. The Criminal Investigation Division occupied that entire floor up there on that side overlooking

Main Street. And that division was paralyzed trying to answer other crimes that occurred in the city. But nonetheless, there was this one little reporter who was shorter than myself, who always kept jumping up trying to get above the heads of everybody else in the hallway, and he always called Fritz "Sheriff." Remember? He says, "Sheriff, I demand an answer." What do you think that did to Will Fritz? Any other questions?

Wes Wise:[16] There was no question there became quite a bit of competition between the local press and the out-of-town and out-of-country press, and I was president of the Press Club that year and we were besieged by the Dallas—then-called oligarchy—to do whatever we could to try to "accommodate the visiting press." And so we had to walk that very tight line and I remember getting together with Tom Simmons and I believe Charlic Dameron, who were former presidents of the Press Club. We all got together and we said, "Look, what can we do that will help to accommodate the

visiting press and yet not be public relations people for the City of Dallas."

And it was a very tight, very tight line to try to walk. I felt we did it pretty well, but I'll have to say to you that the very thing that one of the newspapermen spoke of here where some of the visiting press literally stole some of the material from the newspapers, the same thing happened with the radio and television stations. I have to say to you that I think the visiting press

Wise

were so anti-Dallas at that time that probably nothing would have accommodated them. And it really got under our skin, and especially mine as somebody who was going to be a future official for the City of Dallas—I didn't know that then, obviously, that they would—that we would—befriend them and try to help them and that would turn around on us and

[16]A radio and television reporter for KRLD-TV and Radio who later was elected mayor of Dallas for three terms in 1971, 1973 and 1975.

blast us. Especially blast our citizens. I thought that was something that was very important.

I know some of the visiting press took credit for things that the local press had actually accomplished. For instance, Bob Huffaker and Tom Petit were the only ones who had the live telecasts of the—or telecasts I should say from the basement of the city hall of Ruby shooting Oswald. Well, sort of like all those people who say they had the first announcement of the death of President Kennedy, after it came out in the various reports and newspapers and so forth, you would have thought every television newsman in the country had covered the Ruby shooting live on television. So that was something that I thought would kind of—I think the fact that there was a real competition between local press and both out-of-city and out-of-the-country press was very important at that time.

Ewell: Thank you, Wes.

Tinsley: Jim, it seemed for weeks after that when new reporters would come in from the *New York Times* or some of the national newspapers or overseas, one of the first things they would do would be to identify reporters who had covered various aspects of the story and they would come and interview you, and in effect, debrief you.

This went on for quite a while, and it was during that period of time—I'm sure this may have happened at other newspapers, too—that we were pretty lax in the way we ran what we then called the morgue—now it's called the reference room—and as a result of that, a lot of things disappeared. If we had known then what we knew later we would have put a clamp on that reference room from the very beginning. But we didn't, and we lost a lot of stuff, and I'm sure that this may have been happening at other newspapers and other news organizations.

Ewell: Thank you, Jack. And I think it's also going to be important to note here before we dismiss this panel . And Jack and Bill Winfrey's arrival, and introduce Bill Winfrey back to the audience. But another thing to remember—that no American city had ever experienced what was happening to Dallas as a result of that thunderbolt. The officialdom, the Dallas Police Department, and anything else did not have the mechanisms in place that they have now for dealing with the media. As a result of what took place in November of 1963 I think it set in motion, it began adding to the press department, law enforcement department, the Pentagon and everything else, adding into it press relations departments, press relations officers. I tell you, I think that was the spin that came out of Dallas, and as a result of that our law enforcement across the country and everything else is more prepared to handle major cosmetic situations. From there we went to Memphis, Tennessee, and then to Los Angeles and everything else. How much better did they handle it after the Dallas experience?

Let me introduce to you now again who has been on one panel previously, but Bill Winfrey was everywhere as a cameraman, spot news, and everything else, we know that and everything else, but I'd like for you to hear from Bill how we had to compete with that situation that existed between the presidential assassination and the killing of the man accused of killing the president.

Winfrey: Let me apologize for not being in my place here. They moved me to an earlier panel and they didn't tell me that I was going to get to do it twice. So I went to lunch.

The thing I remember most about the congestion and as the hours went by on Friday more and more and more people came from out of town. We had a certain protocol and respect for our fellow photographers, our—we didn't interfere with anything, we didn't get in front of anybody, we had a certain politeness—we had to work with them again. And this was formidable, tough guys here—Pete Fisher and Jerry McNeill and this rascal here. If you got in front of them and did anything wrong you might answer for it. We all of a sudden were inundated with people that had a complete hatred for us. We were Dallas, we were part of the plan. These—I call them the Yankee press—the Northern press came in and there was a thing which I had never dealt with. I had been all over the country, and in the ensuing months I was assigned to [President Lyndon B.] Johnson, and I would go down to the ranch every time he did, and we rented a motel room in the Stonewall motels. Every time he moved I did, and Ferd [Kaufman] and I almost lived down there, and some of the other AP boys they had a room down there, too.

So we still worked with each other, and we helped each other. We all had a common goal to do our job. So we had some problems. We didn't dare set a camera down. We didn't set a camera bag down. You didn't do anything that you didn't watch every minute, and I'm sure some of the rest of you will remember—you protected your stuff, and it was different. The people that were there—there were little clusters here and little clusters here and us over here, and you could try to talk to them. It wasn't the same. We ended up in the same little bunches. Some of them were big name people and some were not.

But in the next few days I worked all day Friday, Friday night, Saturday I did not go home until Saturday some time late in the afternoon. I was still wearing the same clothes I had left home with to cover the luncheon on Friday morning. I went to the paper and turned out some film and went right back, and I spent the night there.

We just didn't know what was going to happen, and it was mind-boggling the proportion of the story that was—it began to soak in, I think, the next day, what had really happened, and I've covered all kinds of news stories for many years and never had a thought about it, but the responsibility of every single thing you do, every picture, every frame becomes very, very important, and it was probably a day later that I really realized had I done this or had I done that and I didn't get this. The paper depended upon us, and I'd like to publicly say one thing here. I worked for many years with Tom Dillard and Clint Grant and ten other photographers—there were twelve to thirteen of us—the things I learned and the things I did, the pictures I made, the responsibility that I accepted, the responsibility I hope I fulfilled, and then assigned with the White House press later and all this is directly responsible to these guys. Everyone of them shared in everything I learned, because when I started there I didn't know nothing. From Jerry McNeill—I knew him back when he had hair—almost. But these people, we were a fraternal order with responsibility to the public to present the news and not make the news and today I'm sort of a speechmaker. Today I see a different period. The Geraldos [Rivera] just make me sick.

Ewell: The next person who has asked to say just a word was the farm editor covering agriculture news, and I think he was probably the only resident Aggie[17] on the *Dallas News* staff at that time. Aggie-in-residence. Tom Milligan.

Milligan: Thank you, Jim. I apologize to you right now about that crack about your hair. Mine turned white and yours turned loose. The subject of out-of-town press is a subject close to my heart. I wouldn't have gone home that Friday if I could have. I had ridden with Jack Krueger's secretary, Maurine Lovell, God rest her soul, but nevertheless. I was not an investigative reporter, I had no assignment like [Hugh] Aynesworth said.

Milligan

Anyway, back to this point of out-of-town press. Along about 6 or 7 p.m. Mr. Krueger sent Mrs. Lovell out to get me a thing from Buster Haas' desk where I said, "What can I do other than stay out of your way?" And Buster said write photo captions—cutlines we called them, and don't bother me. I said if you don't know something make it up. We've got to move it on AP wire. You see, Joe Dealey had already said, no blood money. Now, I'll get to that later when we get on to this—I think I'm on that sidebar panel. But he assigned me to take care of the out-of-town press. Find them a desk, a telephone, et cetera. By 7 or 8 o'clock the *New York*

---

[17] A nickname for graduates of Texas A&M.

Times had over a dozen people, including their head deskman, I'll never forget his name: Fendell Yerxia of Washington, D.C.

I put them in the women's news department. It had a rim and slot and all that business, and somebody had the audacity to say did you call Katie Dillard[18], Tom's wife, and get her permission. I said, "You've got to be kidding. I'm a mean damn Aggie and Krueger said get it done."

So we had people including a few of our own, maybe two or three, and I'll not call names because I might miss somebody, that robbed the morgue, our morgue. I caught one and I know there were more. This was before we put the guard on the gate. But the *Kansas City Times, Kansas City Star*, I can't remember his name because he used to cover agricultural events with him and I almost did bodily harm to him.

They headed first for General [Edwin A.] Walker's file,[19] some of them did. And a whole drawer on that old dude that is buried down south of Kerrville a couple of weeks ago where I now live in Kerrville. But the majority on Friday night, Saturday night, and Sunday night of the out-of-town press at the *News* that showed us proper credentials and Mary Elizabeth Woods spoke Spanish and we finally found her to talk to some Mexican journalists that I guarantee you looked like Pancho Villa's boys, and they finally put a guard on the back elevator. We had a bomb threat.

But anyway, for that weekend I observed a large amount of ethics in journalism from the big majority, and we had a mob of them at the *Dallas News*. I don't know how many Charlie [Dameron] and them had at the *Herald*. And I'm not here to defend or condemn anyone, but we found a typewriter and paper and telephone. Of course, you didn't have direct-distance dialing. The *Dallas News* had one helluva switchboard operation. . .

---

[18] Women's editor of the *Dallas Morning News*.

[19] Walker had settled in Dallas after resigning his commission in the U.S. Army when he came under intense scrutiny for allegedly indoctrinating troops under his command with right-wing political material. In Dallas he had continued to make news with his political pronouncements.

Ewell: Amen

Milligan: and I doubt any of you—he said amen. I didn't know you were religious.

Ewell: On that score I am.

Milligan: But you know, that *New York Times,* and I saw Tom Wicker on that Channel 4 [KDFW] or [Dan] Rather's program last night. I'm pretty sure Tom was with that bunch. I forget how we looked. I thought Winfrey and Ewell were pink-faced kids back then. I was the tender age of 37. Why, hell, most of them are just three or four years younger than me, but it's that respect that—Tom Dillard wants to raise his hand, but I'm not going to let you talk because this is the boss. I—he's 85 or going on a 100, I think.

But the out-of-town press. I don't know about later on, because you know, blood money chasing money, some reporters chasing good stories, some of them chasing books, and all these innuendoes. I volunteered to go on the Warren Commission because I met Senator—is it Congressman or Senator?—Gerald Ford[20] at Chicago's Farm Bureau Convention, and an ABC-TV guy jumped right in at the first question and said, "Do you ever expect the Dallas police department to cooperate with you?" And bless Mr. Ford's heart. He stuttered and stammered. I jumped up. I was on the edge like hell, it was like a week or ten days since the president was killed. And I kind of half hollered out, "Have they cooperated up till now?" And this ABC-TV Chicago boy stuck that mike, "Who are you and who do you represent?" And I said, "None of your G.D. business." And Ford—so I apologized to him, but he thanked me for getting him off the hook.

But it was that kind of—you know—Jules Duscha from that same weekend from the *Washington Post* who wrote a book about Billie Sol Estes and Winfrey and I slept together

---

[20]Ford was then a Republican Congressman from Michigan, an appointed member of the Warren Commission.

with Jimmy Banks during the Billie Sol scandal. We were in his office all day before he was arrested. I mean we had separate beds, you understand.

Ewell: Another story, Tom. Okay.

Milligan: But Jules Duscha jumped up at a cocktail party on Sunday night and hollered at me, "You son of a bitch from the *Dallas News*. You killed our president." And I tried to kill him. The president of the American Farm Bureau held me back. That was the syndrome. Thank you.

Ewell: Well, there you have it from this panel. And I thank you very much.

JACK RUBY:
A SHOCKING TURN

TONY ZOPPI, Moderator

It was wildly improbable that the accused assassin could be in danger when he was to be transferred from the temporary city jail to the more permanent county jail; yet, while handcuffed to a detective he was shot and killed by nightclub owner Jack Ruby amidst a crowd of journalists and police officers. (This session began at 2:15 p.m. and ended at 3:15 p.m.)

Payne: Two weeks after Pearl Harbor, Tony Zoppi, a young New Jersey lad, enlisted in the U.S. Army. Eventually, he was assigned to Longview, Texas, where he met and married a Longview native. And thus, Tony became a Texan. Tony began his journalism career at the *Longview News-Journal*. He covered general assignments, sports, and the night life (such as there was in Longview). In 1948 he found himself in Canton, Texas, covering a speech made by senatorial candidate Lyndon Baines Johnson. The story caught Johnson's eye, and Tony accepted an offer to join the Johnson team as an advance publicist.

This work led to an offer from the *Dallas Morning News*, which he accepted in 1950. For the first two years there he was a sportswriter, then he transferred to the amusements department. For nearly fifteen years Tony covered the national entertainment scene, ranging from the Copacabana in New

York City to the Coconut Grove in Los Angeles. He became friendly with some of the biggest stars in show business. His column, "Dallas After Dark," was a must-read.

In 1965 Tony accepted an offer from the Riviera Hotel in Las Vegas to be director of publicity and advertising. Soon he was promoted to vice president in charge of entertainment. He booked such stars as Frank Sinatra, Liza Minelli, Dolly Parton, Dean Martin, Shirley Maclaine, Kenny Rogers, and many others.

He returned to Dallas in 1982 to operate his own entertainment booking agency.

He says that the most memorable portions of his career involved his coverage of the Kennedy assassination and his friendship with the rather crude owner of a small nightclub who seemed desperate to be like the big-time stars Tony knew but who was himself hopelessly small-time. His name was Jack Ruby.

And now, to moderate the panel discussion on events that included Jack Ruby's elevation to national headlines, Tony Zoppi.

Zoppi: Thank you, Darwin. Well, it's great to be here, and I'm amazed at the magnificent job everyone did—especially Darwin in getting this thing on because as recently as a week ago it was really touch and go. We had very few tickets sold and it was kind of scary. But this turnout has been just great— very heartening.

I met Jack Ruby twelve years before the assassination. A friend of mine by the name of Matty Brescia, who was publicist for the old Liberty Network owned by Gordon McLendon, came to my office and said, "You got to meet this guy. He's a real character from Chicago. His name is Jack Ruby."

And he was over at Bob Wills' ranch house. I think he had a little piece of that place. And we went in—the place probably sat between 800 and a thousand people—and there were somewhere around fifteen or twenty people in the audience, and I was seated at the front row, and he gave me a very flowery introduction. He was always groping for big words, telling how superfluous it was to have Tony Zoppi in the audience. And the minute he got through he jumped off-stage and came down to my table and said, "Do you know Kup?" And that was Irv Kupcinet, a legend in journalism in the Chicago area. And of course I knew Kup. We had been on many trips together. And then he asked me if I knew Dinje and Donjo and so forth and so on. Well, I found out years later that Dinje and Donjo owned a very famous nightclub in Chicago called the Chez Paree, and I worked with Dinje Halper at the Riviera Hotel.

But he was a name-dropper, and as I got to know him through the years he would come by the office seeking plugs for his various nightclubs, and when he took over the Carousel which was known as the Sovereign Club before it became the Carousel, he was always asking me for plugs.

One day he walked in and said, "Let me see your fingernails." I showed him my fingernails and he said, "Look at my fingernails. Aren't they beautiful?" I said, "Yeah, mine are very fragile, actually." He said, "I'm going to bring you something that will give you beautiful fingernails." And the next day he brought this carton up to the office and dumped it down on my desk, and there was a caseful of gelatin. He said, "Put a teaspoonful of that in your coffee every morning and you'll have beautiful fingernails like mine." And I used about two spoonfuls of it and I never used it again. But this was typical. One day he had pizza ovens. The day he had skating boards. He was always into something.

Much has been said about my relationship with Jack Ruby, especially by some of the authors who are trying to prove a conspiracy. One of them in particular, whose book and name I will not use because I don't want anybody buying the book. He asked me to sue him because I think he was looking for publicity. But he insinuated that Jack, of course, was part of the conspiracy and I was providing an alibi for him, and a lot of it revolved around the fact that I was supposed to go to Cuba with Jack. The reason Jack Ruby was in Cuba was because he stopped me on the street one day—on Commerce Street—and he said, "How would you like to go to Havana?"

In those days I was traveling constantly, going all over the country, covering shows. And I had never been to Havana, and I said, "Yeah, I'd like to go." So he said, "Well, Lou McWilly," who was a gambler here in Dallas in the old days whom I had never met. I don't ever remember meeting Lou McWilly, but I knew him by name. He said, "Lou is head of the casino at the Tropicana in Havana." He said, "I was talking to him and he said he wants you to come down and write a story about their show." So I went back to the *News* and I talked with Jack Krueger, and Jack was very liberal about me taking trips as long as it didn't cost the *Dallas News* anything. They gave me twenty dollars expense money on every trip I ever took, and of course my hosts in Las Vegas gave me free room, food and beverage. So actually, the cost to me was minimal, but I considered it an investment in my career.

So I told him I would go to Cuba with him. And we set the date in the early part of December. And in the meantime, I had done a promotion for the Sands Hotel on my television show in which we solicited young girls, Texas girls, who wanted to be chorus girls in Las Vegas. And they were going to audition on my television show, and Jack Entratter, the president of the Sands, would come down and pick the winners. He selected fourteen girls, took them back to Las Vegas, and transformed them into gorgeous chorus girls. So, after I told Ruby I would go to Havana with him, which was in November, and we set the date for December, Entratter called me and said, "You gotta come out to the Sands because we've got Nat Cole, we've got Rowan and Martin, who were very good friends of mine, and your Texas Copa girls."

So I called Jack and said, "Listen, I've got to postpone the trip. I want to go out to Vegas and see this show." So he said, "Well when do you want to go?" I said, "Let's go the first weekend after the first of the year, about the fourth of January." "OK," he says, "but I'm going to go on ahead." I said, "Fine, I'll see you down there on the fourth." Well, as we all know, Castro moved in on the first of January, and that was the end of that. But he was in Cuba. He had gone down ahead. And Lou McWilly said that he was the biggest pain-in-the-neck. He stayed down there for ten days, and the fact that I didn't go—they refused to pay his plane fare and his hotel room. But he did go back another time.

But they're trying to make a connection, and insinuated that I was part of the Mafia because I was supposed to go to Cuba with Ruby. And this is the way some of these people who write these books have no regard for character or anything that will make a story, they don't care. And, I went on the Geraldo [Rivera] show if you'll pardon the expression, simply because this author was going to be on it. When I heard he was going to be on it I went up there and I cornered him in the dressing room, and I told him what I thought of him. And he became even more vicious after that. And he's really done a number on me. But I know who I am, and it doesn't bother me.

I kept this panel down numerically because I wanted to give each of us a little longer time to talk. I'm going to tell one or two Ruby stories.

After he shot Oswald he called me from his jail cell a couple of days afterwards and I was having lunch at the King's Club. The manager told me was on the phone so I talked to him in generalities for a few minutes. And I said, "Jack, why the hell did you do it?" And he started to cry. And he said, "I didn't want Jackie to have to come down here and stand trial against that Commie rat. And those poor kids left without a father." He said, "I was raised without a father, and I know what they're going . . ." And I said, "Wait a minute, wait a minute, Jack." I said, "You can't compare yourself with the Kennedy children." I said, "As horrible as this thing was they're not going to have to scrounge the way you did."

And then he really started crying, and he said, "I've got to tell you something I've never told anyone." And I figured here it comes, if he was involved in any kind of conspiracy, now he was going to confess to me. Because we were really good friends. He said, "There is an orphanage over in Oak Cliff, and every Christmas I bring every kid in that orphanage"—now it's a Catholic orphanage and he's Jewish—and he brought every kid in that orphanage a Christmas present. I don't know how many years. And he even brought presents to the nuns. He said, "Here it's going to be Christmas this year and nobody is going to get a gift." And it really tore him up.

He was crying and all of a sudden he stopped abruptly and said, "And I wanted to prove there was one Jew with guts." And it was such a confusing conversation I couldn't make heads nor tails of it.

But this was typical Jack Ruby. He was very hyper, and he had a giggle when he would come to my office and tell a story. He would start giggling with this shrill giggle. The people I worked with in the office, they'd say, "How do you tolerate that guy?" And I said, "To me, he's a letter from home because I'm from the Jersey shore and I knew a bunch of guys just like him that hung around the pool room and they were all cut from the same mold. It's just a type, and he was that type.

One quick story about Melvin Belli,[1] who no one has mentioned. I got a phone call from a producer in Hollywood by the name of Gene Mann, and he said, "Tony, Mel Belli is coming down there to handle the Jack Ruby case. Pick him up at the airport and show him the town. He loves night clubs." So I met him and I took him around and all he did was blast the *Dallas News*. Every day he would just take the *Dallas News* apart, and the oligarchy.

So one day told him, I said, "Mel, you're going to keep doing this, I can't hang out with you." He said, "Don't you know why I'm doing this?" And I said, "No." He said, "I want to get this case transferred out of Dallas. I want a change of venue. I'd love to try it in Fort Worth. They haven't convicted anyone there in a hundred years." So he tried a change of venue and it was turned down. But we became very friendly during the course of the trial, and he was an unforgettable character.

And I was with Jack's family at the sentencing, the day Judge Brown sentenced him to death, and that was a very traumatic time. I think I've used up just about all of my time. I had several other stories but these people have some better ones.

---

[1] Belli was the flamboyant and widely publicized attorney from San Francisco who represented Ruby in his trial for shooting Oswald.

I want to introduce Bob Jackson, who you met earlier. And Bob if you can say a few words, and please keep the microphone in close because I understand that they can't hear too well.

Jackson. Can you hear this from the back? Well, my assignment on Sunday was to photograph the transfer of Lee Harvey Oswald from the city jail to the county jail. And they

Jackson

had given us a tentative time when they would move him. And so I remember going down that Sunday morning, no traffic on the road to speak of, and I was going down Ross Avenue. I was the only car on the road, and then I saw this truck coming toward me, and just as he got past me he backfired, and then after the two previous days I was kind of a basketcase anyway. But this tremendous backfire, and it just had me thinking all over again about Friday and being in the motorcade.

Anyway, when I got to the police station I went up to the press room. There was no security to speak of. No one checked my credentials or anything. I went up to the press room and eventually we realized that we weren't going to be able to—that they weren't going to transfer him when they originally said. But finally they took the newsmen down to the basement, and we still didn't know how long it would be before they brought him down. Finally, they did say that they would be bringing him down momentarily. We were to pick a spot that we would shoot from and stay there. Now in the basement there were two—well, there was an armored carrier that they had started to back down the ramp. And it would not clear the entrance, the top was too high. So they left it at the top of the ramp. And then they brought in two unmarked cars, I believe, two or three, I believe it was two, and they were lined up and the news media—we were all in a kind of—well, grouped around a little open area.

And so I felt like I should pick a spot where I could get the best picture, and my idea was to focus, pre-focus on a spot about ten feet away. It was a pretty routine assignment really. We had shot prison transfers before. It was not an unusual situation except for the people involved. So I picked my place, and I remember Frank Johnson was standing right next to me— UPI photographer. And, Jack Beers [of the *Dallas Morning News*] was a little further to the right and he was standing up on a little wall to get a high angle. The AP photographer was somewhere up the ramp, close to the armored vehicle. I think his idea was to get a picture of Oswald being put in the van, assuming he was going to be put in the van.

So, they told us that they were bringing him down and so we all got ready and I had pre-focused. I was looking through the camera. They brought him out into the open space. And my plan was to shoot a frame there and then back up the ramp as far as I could go and continue shooting whatever I could get as they put him in one of the cars, one of the vehicles So, as he stepped into the clear space I was aware of someone [Jack Ruby] stepping out in front of me to block my view, and I remember leaning a little bit over the fender of the car. Frank Johnson was crowding me on the right, and it all happened very fast. He [Ruby] only took maybe two steps and brought his arm up. I was fortunate that I was already looking through the camera. If I had not been looking through the camera, I would have had to react to the shooting and bring the camera up I wouldn't have gotten the shot I got. So, he fired and I fired almost simultaneously.

And then all hell broke loose. One policeman I remember running up over the police car, over the hood, over the top, down the trunk and into the pile as they were wrestling Ruby to the ground. I shot another frame right away but I knew my strobe would not recycle that fast. It would take me about six seconds to recycle, so I knew it would be a dark frame. But I shot anyway. And then the next thing was a policeman with his hand on my camera shoving me back along with the other newsmen. So we had that to contend with. So finally after they had removed both Ruby and Oswald into the building, then we were kept there until they brought an ambulance in and transported Oswald. I got another picture of Oswald being put in the ambulance.

So then I recall we had to stay down there in the basement for a while, a good while before we were even allowed to go up into the building. And I went and called the paper and told them I felt like I had something good. I wasn't sure exactly what it was going to look like.

So, to make a long story short, about two hours later I was able to go back to the paper after they sent another photographer to relieve me, and I went back to the paper to process my film. And our chief photographer [John Mazziotta] was standing right outside the door. Well, first of all, when I came into the building, when I came into the newsroom, everybody was gathered around the wire machine looking at Jack Beers' picture that was taken maybe a second before mine. And somebody said, "Do you have anything this good?" Everybody was really on edge. So I said I'll let you know in a minute.

So I went in and processed my film and I remember letting out a big yell. And our chief photographer, he ran out to the newsroom and said, "We've got something good." "Well, bring me a print." So we made a wet print and carried it out there and passed it around, showed everybody and then we got busy making some good prints and then the rest of the day was—I can't remember much about it really. But I went home with a big headache that night, I'll tell you.

Zoppi: He also went home with a Pulitzer Prize. That's one of the great pictures of all time, and that ought to be around for hundreds of years. Our next panelist, whom you've met earlier, is Wes Wise, who knew Jack Ruby quite well, and—oh, I want to correct one thing that I said this morning—that I went up to the Adolphus Hotel with an FBI man by the name of Will Griffith. Somebody said I said Will Fritz. It was Will Griffith—was the FBI man that we went to the Adolphus with.[2] OK, here's Wes.

---

[2] In his earlier comments on the panel, "Fateful Moments," Zoppi erroneously referred to Griffiths as Fritz. See Page 73.

Wise: I'm going to come away from the basement of the Dallas city hall because it has been widely publicized in various books and so forth that I met Jack Ruby at the School Book Depository Building, which I did the day *after* the assassination at about 1:30 p.m. News director Eddie Barker had sent me there to try to retrace Lee Harvey Oswald's steps all the way from the sixth floor down to catching the bus, getting the cab, going across to the bus stop, going back to his rooming house, etc., etc. And in that procedure I had parked the KRLD News station wagon, which of course had "KRLD News" on the side of it, cater-cornered on what is I guess Houston Street, but then was not open from Elm on back north, I suppose.

As I sat there on the two-way radio back to the base station I reported back to Jim Underwood, the assistant news director, that I had gotten pictures in the sixth floor, had gotten into the building, had gotten pictures in the sixth floor and now was going to be en route to Oak Cliff to try to retrace Lee Harvey Oswald's steps. And as I did I saw a figure out of the corner of my eye running from back where the railroad tower is behind the School Book Depository Building, back from that direction. I remember later thinking why he was back there instead of in front of the building where most of the crowd was. And he knocked on the mirror—I mean the window—and I lowered the window and it was Jack Ruby.

And he was excitable, always was excitable, but he was especially excitable at this time. He said, "Oh, isn't this a terrible thing that has happened?" And I agreed with him and I told him that during the course of an eight- to ten-minute conversation that the previous day following the assassination I had taken pictures of the western saddles which the City of Dallas was going to give to the Kennedys to take to Caroline and John-John. And when I did tears visibly came to his eyes. And for that reason I was called as a witness in the Ruby trial both for the defense, on one occasion, and for the prosecution on another occasion.

It was immediately reported that after I had reported to KRLD—well, let me go forward on that—after Ruby had shot Oswald I then gave a report to KRLD that I had seen Ruby at the School Book Depository Building on Saturday—that's Friday, the day of the assassination. This was on Saturday, and then Sunday was the day that Ruby shot Oswald. Mal Couch, who was a very capable reporter—but I don't know how he got that information wrong—he was quoted as saying, on Associated Press, I believe, or on one of the news services that I had said I had seen Jack Ruby at the School Book Depository Building on the day of the assassination. And I've had real difficulty down through the years straightening that out. In fact, two authors of two of the major books on the assassination have reported that I saw Jack Ruby at the School Book Depository Building on the day of the assassination, which I would repeat, is not correct. It's interesting to point out, however, that the authors of those books never called me. Nor have I been called by any authors of any books, although I've been quoted in these books repeatedly, I've never been called by any author of any book. And these two books that erroneously reported that I had seen Jack Ruby on the day of the assassination, they never called me or interviewed me or checked.

Back in these journalists' days you always had to check at least two sources was the rule I always lived by, and preferably three, but never did you accept just a single source. And again, the authors of some of the books are just not doing that. That's about as—as far as Jack Ruby and his temperament, it's just as Tony pointed out, as a sports broadcaster he would be at almost every boxing match I ever attended. He would be at every football game, maybe not every baseball game, but every—of various sporting events, but on some of the hard news stories. He'd be at fires, he'd be at major accidents, he was a real newsman groupie, and then after that I think he was probably a policeman groupie, too, a police station groupie from what I've learned. But his temperament.

Zoppi: Wes, can I say something?

Wise: Sure, sure.

Zoppi: Maybe you saw it on the Dan Rather show last night. They quoted me, and my first comment was, "He [Ruby] was like horse manure. He was all over." He didn't miss a trick. Anything going on in town, he was there.

Wise: One more thing. On the security in the Dallas city hall. I think we're making a real mistake for some of the younger generation who weren't even born at the time of the assassination. You must realize that security in 1963 wasn't anything even remotely resembling what security is in 1993. If I wanted to go up and see the sports editor of the *Dallas Morning News*, I simply pushed the button of the elevator and went to the desk of the sports editor. If I wanted to go up and see Tony Zoppi I just went up in the elevator and saw Tony Zoppi at his desk. Now, you have to sign in and sign out, you have a badge and so forth, and you do the same thing at most government buildings today. You've got to remember when you think of the lack of security in Dallas city hall, which was also the jail, of course, where Oswald was taken first. You've got to remember that security then was not what security is today, and it's got to be taken in that context.

Zoppi: Thank you. Our next guest came down here from New York to attend this panel, and we're very honored to have him here. He was with station WNEW in New York at the time of the assassination, and he struck up an acquaintance with Jack Ruby down in the jail in the city hall area. He went on to become a household word in the television medium. All of us have seen him many times on television, one of the great commentators. Ike Pappas.

Pappas: Thanks. And I have to say immediately and offer my thanks to Darwin Payne and SMU for staging this event because I think educationally it's extraordinarily important for students of the future to understand and to get our personal perspectives in order for them to totally understand what went on during that weekend and also afterwards. And what Wes just said is perfectly accurate—that security was nothing like what it is today because the Kennedy assassination set off, or rather preceded a whole series of events and other assassinations and sensitized this country and the whole world to the lack of security that existed in those days. And it's an entirely different picture today.

I am happy to see all of you again after thirty years. It's astounding to me how much you've all aged, while I have stayed, I have stayed relatively the same.

Pappas

I want to tell the story real fast because we want to keep it moving. I'll give you sort of not the long version and not the short version but the medium version because, believe me, I've told it many, many times as we all have over thirty years of lectures, and I get requests to do seminars such as this about this story and I'm fairly well practiced at it.

I was not in Dallas the day the president was shot, or at the moment the president was shot. I was on vacation—a day off—a vacation day, from my assignment as a reporter for WNEW Radio. And I decided that morning to go down to see my dentist, "Painless" Pete Cutross, and to get that done and to go down to Greenwich Village and have some lunch with some friends and maybe buy some Christmas cards and so forth.

And I took this subway to West Fourth Street. Came out of the subway in New York City and a woman came up to me immediately, and she was screaming and crying. Her face, I recall, was matted down with hair, wet hair, and her face glistened with tears, and she was screaming at me that the president has been shot, the president has been shot! And cynical—I was pretending to be cynical in those days as a young, cynical reporter—and I said to myself, when the tourists come out tonight, lady, you can tell them that story. I don't believe it.

But then I looked around and there was an electricity in the air. And New Yorkers were doing something they never do— they were talking to each other. They were stopping and listening to radios that they had, and I suddenly got terrorized and said, "What if it's true?" I ran across the street, put a nickel in the coin box, the telephone box—it was a nickel in those days, remember—and I called my office. I did not have to ask the question, What about Kennedy? But as soon as the phone was answered—"Hello, Newsroom,"—and I heard this enormous rush—teletype machines, people screaming, telephones, my heart sank. And I said into the phone, "What's this about Kennedy?" And the guy, and this is an accurate quote, said, "Get your ass up here." Historically, I have to tell you that. Whether it's worth anything, that's what he said, and I slammed the phone down and my immediate response was, "Goddammit, they got him."

And if you recall all of the pre-publicity about this trip to Texas. That it was unsafe, shouldn't go. Civil rights problems.[3] You know, don't go down there. Everybody was saying is it going to happen? Is something going to happen to the president? And we in the news business in New York were talking about that possibility. And I felt that at that point that he was done in by extremists, by segregationists—I don't know, for lack of a better label. I grabbed a cab and went uptown, and in a pit ride I can tell you about briefly. Talk about the cynicism of New York City cab drivers, the phone—rather, the radio was not on and I jumped in the cab and said, "Turn on the radio, turn on the radio." And he says "What's going on? What's wrong?" And I said, "Well, didn't you hear? The president has been shot." And no expression of sympathy from this cabdriver. Nothing like, not even a gee whiz. And he turned around and he said, "You mean I got to worry about that guy Lyndon Johnson now?" That was his only thought. "And we have to deal with Lyndon Johnson now?" That was like, "What is he going to do with me?"

---

[3] The widespread concern in Dallas, especially noted by its civic and political leaders, was that the incident in which United Nations Ambassador Adlai Stevenson had been confronted rudely a month earlier would be repeated with the president. In that incident, occurring at Dallas Memorial Auditorium on United Nations Day, protesters had disrupted Stevenson's speech. Afterwards, outside the auditorium, demonstrators again confronted him. He was spat upon and hit on the head with a picket sign. Newsreel footage and photographs of this incident were seen across the nation.

I got to WNEW, walked into the—*ran* into the newsroom and was handed fifty, a hundred—I forget what it was—five hundred dollars and a tape recorder and they said, "Get to Dallas. We don't care how you get there."

I ran downstairs, hailed a cab, gave the guy twenty dollars, and took then the most fantastic ride, one of the most fantastic taxi rides ever because if you'll recall New York City was in a state of shock with the rest of the world, and the bridges were jammed. The telephones—you couldn't make a call—you couldn't get out of the city, and I just kept giving this guy twenty-dollar bills and I said, "Get there, man, anyway you can." We went over backyards, through laundry, piles of laundries, rushing out to the airport. And I'm trying to figure out, what the hell am I going to do now? Who's going to Dallas now? I said, Delta Airlines has got to be going to Dallas. They fly to Dallas.

So we went to the Idlewild Airport terminal, and I went running in. Had the guy wait, and the guy said the whole airport is paralyzed. We are not taking off. The government has shut down all transportation. But, he said, I understand a flight is leaving. A special flight is going from American Airlines. So I ran back, went to American Airlines and indeed, they were preparing an airplane which was supposed to go to California, and they just told all the early passengers, you're not going, the FBI and the Secret Service are taking this plane. And is using it. Sorry, you'll have to wait til the airport opens.

So I managed to get on that airplane, loaded very quickly with FBI and Secret Service people, and as many newspeople as could possibly get on, and then it took off without waiting for anybody. And I remember Bob Considine being on it, and I think Jimmy Breslin and a few other big-time New York correspondents and little old me with my tape recorder. A very dramatic flight.

And I want to get to the main part of this, but I won't tell you about the flight, but we were told about the portions of the story that we did not know. By the time I got on the airplane I knew the president was dead. I was handed, also, by the way, this piece of copy and a bunch of UPI and AP copy. And it is the bulletin, Merriman Smith's bulletin, which I still have preserved. "President Kennedy and Governor John Connally of Texas have been cut down by assassin's bullets. They were shot as they toured downtown Dallas in an open car," etc., etc. He dictated that from the top of his head, and by the time I got to the newsroom this was given to me and a stack of other copy and the tape recorder, and off I went.

And all the way down in the airplane we could hear as the airplane flew over a city of large enough size the pilot would pick out of the air the radio reports and pipe them into our cabin. So we knew about Lee Harvey Oswald, we knew about Tippit, we knew all—the Mexican border was closed, we knew about the tension in the country. And by the time we landed in Dallas at Love Field at 8 o'clock that evening after flying to Washington from New York to pick up other Secret Service people, and FBI agents. Stopped there and then went straight down to Dallas.

We got off at about 8 o'clock, and we were pretty much ready and briefed to cover the story. I went right to the police station, and began covering the story, waiting for Oswald to come out. I was there when they held the rifle up, and I was amazed that they were out there showing this rifle to everybody. I mean in New York City they would never do that to a piece of evidence. They would be looking at it, protecting it, and here walking down the hall was a detective holding this thing up in the air, and that astounded me. And they expected Ruby—rather Oswald—to come out at various times, and I recall filing several stories and then hearing a lot of the reporters say—not so much the Dallas reporters—but the out-of-town reporters and also the foreign reporters who were there from New York City and from Washington who had arrived with us and had gotten here somehow—starting to talk already about a conspiracy and also about the possibility that the police were beating Oswald because they'd noticed this cut that he had got and the black eye at the Texas Theater and they were pressuring police to bring Oswald out. "We want to see him. If you're not beating him, why don't you show him to us?"

And I guess they decided about midnight to bring him down because that's exactly what they did. And my theory is that they brought him out simply to prove that he was not being maltreated behind closed doors. And into the lineup room I went, covered the story.

Of course, the deal was that we were not going to ask any questions. Oh, no, no questions. Bring him down. We only want to look at him. And Captain Fritz agreed to that and Jesse Curry did, too. No questions. Of course, as soon as he hit the door everybody asked questions. The rules went out the window. Here he is, the most notorious prisoner in American history, and right in front of us, I'm going to ask this guy a question. And I screamed at him just like everybody else. "Did you shoot the president?" And he didn't answer. He came in, and, "How did you get hurt?" and other questions that were around the periphery. And then everybody said, "Let's ask the same question. Did you shoot the president?" And then he said, "No, that's what I'm accused of. I didn't shoot anybody." And then the rules were broken; they whisked him away.

When the dust cleared Henry Wade, the district attorney of Dallas County, was doing an interview talking to reporters. Now I was desperate for a telephone. Could not find—now, all of the guys in the know, all the local reporters, knew exactly where to go, and I was just out of luck. And I ran out into a room outside of the line-up room, and there I saw some telephones. And I'm dialing New York and I say, "I've got to get Henry Wade on here. I'm going to do an interview with him. After that I can get a fix on the story. Stand by to record, and I'm yelling and looking around frantically like that, and up comes this little guy in a blue suit, much like this one, pin-striped suit with a gray fedora. And he says, "What's the matter?" And I say, "I'm looking for Henry Wade." He said, "What are you, a reporter?" I said, "Yeah." He said, "Where you from?" "New York." I said, "Are you a cop?" Because I thought he was a vice cop. I said, ah, here's a detective. He's got an office. He's got a phone. I've got to humor this guy.

So, he says, "No, my name is Jack Ruby. I run the Carousel Club." I said, "Uh, well, amazing." I said, "Jack Ruby, the Carousel Club. What is it?" He says, "Here, come on." He gives me his card. And he says, "Get some of your guys down after this is over with and come on down and have a beer. We have a lot of girls there, you know. Take care of you." So I played along. I played along, and I said, "OK, I got your card. Right here. Put it right here. Right? OK? Now, I got to have Henry Wade over here. Can you go get him? I got to watch the phone." He said, "Just a minute." He said—no, "Do you want Henry Wade?" I didn't ask him; he said, "Do you want Henry Wade? Hold on." He goes running over to Henry Wade, taps him—he says, "Henry," mumble, mumble, "guy from New York." And Henry looks over and says, "Tell him I'll be right over there."

So, astoundingly, Jack Ruby arranges an interview with Henry Wade, the district attorney of Dallas County. Now I'm saying, "This guy is really wired." And Ruby disappears. And Henry Wade walks over, and I do the interview. And I'm absolutely flabbergasted by all this, but nevertheless I continue. I did a great job on the interview. Everybody is congratulating me. Personal interview with Henry Wade. Blah.

I go to KLIF because we had an arrangement with them. My office in the meantime had told me that we are going to get you a place to work. We need a lot of stuff in the morning. So, I'm working away at KLIF and in comes some—and I'm studying, I'm concentrating on my copy and on my tape recording, and I'm trying to pick out a thing—and I see somebody walk in front of me, somebody, and the next thing I know the engineer is telling me, "Do you want a sandwich? Do you want some coffee?" I said, "Oh, did you order out?" He said, "No, Jack Ruby just brought over some sandwiches." That was, by the way, the sandwiches that Gary [DeLaune] was referring to.[4] We finally got them around 2 o'clock in the morning after he did not find Gary down at the police station and so, "I think I'll bring them to KLIF." So, it was a great sandwich, I'll tell you. And I said, Jack Ruby, there's that weird guy again. Now I made him as a buff, as a police buff. As a—I'm going to hustle this up—as a guy who did hang

---

[4] See page 82.

around fire houses and so for the excitement. So I wrote him off.

The next time I saw Ruby, and here's the climax, was that morning. And I'll get to it. Very quickly. I decided because I knew it was going to be ten o'clock in the morning, I went over there about 9:15 and I practiced running down the steps of the police headquarters from the third floor to the basement because my idea was to interview Oswald as he came out of the detectives' office because everybody was set in the basement, and me and my New York "quickness," I suppose, I was going to be a sharp guy, get a big scoop and interview him upstairs. And I was with Jerry O'Leary who had the same idea of the *Washington Star.* Jeremiah O'Leary practiced running up and down with me. And in case we missed him.

And out comes Oswald at the appointed hour. Well, it was well after 10 o'clock. I guess it was 11:15 or 11:20. And I went forward with my microphone and I said, "Do you have anything to say in. . . ?" and, you know, I got pushed against the wall and they threw Oswald into the elevator and down he went. And my heart with it, because I said I'll never work again in the news business. How stupid could I be? Here's—you know—this prisoner leaving the basement, and I'm not going to get a description of it. How do I, how do I explain this to my boss that I wasn't there?

Flew down the steps, and I was glad that I did because I had practiced it, I knew what the pitfalls were, and nobody stopped me. I was amazed because there wasn't a cop on the steps saying, "Excuse me, where are you running to?" You know. Into the basement, and I looked around because I expected everybody to be dissolved and leaving and taking notes after Oswald had left.

No, he's still being signed out. And I went—I said greatly relieved. I had to find a place in this great crowd to describe this, and I squeezed into this, next to the bumper of the car in which he was to go to the other jail. And I'm squeezing in and squeezing—big elbows out—and I said, God, I got a great shot here. Quote, unquote.

And Oswald starts to come toward us and I did not know it but I stood and squeezed right in front of Jack Ruby who was waiting to shoot him. And here comes Oswald. Everything was very fast—split seconds—Oswald's coming toward me and I went forward with my microphone, and again I said, "Do you have anything to say in your defense?" Now, just as I'm saying that I hear two or three footsteps— plop plop—and this black flash in front of me and I heard a bang and a flash against Oswald's sweater, his blue sweater, I could see the flash. And I looked down and I said, "I've been shot," I said to myself, "I've been shot. I got to close to this one, too close." And I realized I wasn't shot.

But here is Oswald collapsing, moaning, being dragged in. A big fight in front of me, and I said to myself as a reporter, and I hope you students of the future listen to this one. You'll come upon a time when you'll be met with a story like this perhaps, where you have a choice of shutting up, freezing, and doing nothing, or talking or writing and taking notes and being cool. I had that choice. I said to myself, "If you never say anything ever again into a microphone you have to say it now. This is history. You'll be judged on these words. Almost your entire existence." All this is going through my mind in split seconds.

And I said the only thing that I could say which is what I had witnessed in front of me. "Oswald has been shot. A shot rang out. There is a struggle." Now how's that for brilliant reporting, huh? Wow, perceptive reporting. "Oswald has been shot." How did he get that idea? I'm going to wrap up right now. So, I went down and I kept on broadcasting , and I guess I did a fairly good job because it has received several awards and is part of the permanent collection of the Broadcasting Museum and is on permanent display at the Museum of Broadcasting in New York and I'm proud to say that it is also—my notes and so forth are on display here on the "Sixth Floor" [Museum], and a fairly , fairly good job of reporting for a young guy who was under a lot of stress.

Let me just wrap it up by saying two things. A couple of corrections for history's sake. You heard on the tape, "Holy mackerel." Right? I did say those words, and I'm not proud of those words as a reporter, you know, a guy who is supposed to be great with words under stress. "Holy mackerel." Is that a great thing to say? I did say that, I admit it, I'm not proud of it. But I said it way after that event. I was running, my tape recorder was still going—I did not know it was going, and I was simply—as I was running up the steps to the police station to try to get a telephone I was trying to assess what had happened. This enormous story, one little guy with a tape recorder. How am I ever going to dig out of this big hole? And I just said, "Holy mackerel. Unbelievable," saying that to myself. And an editor in New York in the days before we had editorial-editing integrity, I should say, where you have to leave history alone, took that phrase—"Oh, that's a great phrase. Let's put it up in front, right after he was shot"—and therefore has changed broadcasting history. I did not say it at that point.

The last thing was—I ate the sandwiches, 10 o'clock, OK, I think I covered it all. I do have a couple of other things, but they are peripheral, and I thank you. That's my story.

Zoppi: Very good, Ike. Thank you Ike. Thank you very much for coming all the way from New York to attend this thing. [Actually, from Washington, D.C.] Bob Porter and I— Bob was on the *Times Herald*, I was on the *News*, but we were contemporaries and very friendly rivals. Bob worked in the amusements section at the *Herald*; I was in the amusements department at the *News*, and he knew Jack and had a couple of incidents with him. Would you tell them to us, please?

Porter: Yeah, really kind of briefly, and it's like sort of the next verse of the same song in the sense that Jack was known  to almost all of us because he was always hanging around, and as Wes said about the *News*, you could come to the *Times Herald*, push a button and come up to the fourth floor and walk in, and Jack would do that. He would be giving us passes to his club, slapping us on the back one day. The next day he would come storming in because maybe you had run a picture of Tony Bennett on what we called our amusements

Porter

pages in those days and we never ran any pictures of his entertainers, who were strippers and third-rate comics, you know. He was that kind of a character.

The personal involvement was that afternoon we were still busy in our department putting out our Sunday entertainment section when the motorcade came down Main Street which was two blocks over from the *Times Herald* building. We were on the fourth floor. Somebody said, "Oh, there goes the motorcade." We all dashed over to the windows and could just see through an opening there by One Main Place, the motorcade go by, not even sure which vehicle was carrying the president. And sat back down at our desk.

And then just moments later the call came in that something had happened, and so as Charles Dameron, who was one of our editors, talked about this morning, how we were the afternoon newspaper, we still had editions working, so we were really kind of immediately everyone thrown into this process, even the people back in amusements. And it was a big weekend in terms of there was opera performances, there was the symphony performing, theaters were going on. It occurred to one of the editors, and I think it probably was Charlie who came back and said let's check out and see what is the city going to shut down, what's going to happen?

So I began as the movie and theater critic checking primarily with the theaters, and somewhere in this process which I would guess would be maybe an hour after the assassination, one of the phone lines was blinking and I picked it up and it was Jack Ruby, and he was returning a call to Don Safran who was our nightclub columnist. I looked over at Don and Don was on the telephone, and I said, "Well, Don's on the phone, Jack," and he said, "Well, do you know what he was calling about?" And I said, I explained what we were doing—making this survey.

And he said, "Well, what are the nightclub people doing?" And I said, well, I had only heard about a couple of them but the ones I had heard about said they were going to shut down for the weekend. And he said, "Well, what do you think I should do?" And I said, "Well, hell, I don't know, Jack. It's your club; it's your decision." And there was kind of a pause, and he said, "Well, they said they were going to shut down?" And I said, "Well, that's what they told me." He said, "Well, I guess I'd better shut down too." And I said, "OK, I've got two columns here, closed and open. I'm going to put you in the closed column." And he said, "Yeah, yeah," very sort of indifferently. And that was the last of the conversation. I didn't think much of it at the time, of course, because I was talking to a lot of other people.

We were checking around also with the personalities. I remember the actress Joan Crawford was in the city. I got her on the telephone for her comments, etc., etc., so it was quite a shock then two days later when Jack shot Oswald. But then on reflection, not inconsistent with his personality. Either he was all over the spectrum as his trips to the office illustrated, and so I just thought this little incident might help put his personality profile maybe into a little sharper focus.

Zoppi: Thank you. I forgot all about Joan Crawford being here that day, because I went down to the Statler Hotel and interviewed her, and that night, a fellow I think by the name of Bob Clarey. He was a little Frenchman that appeared in "Hogan's Heroes," he was opening that night at the Statler, so I went down there, and just before show time Joan Crawford walked in with Richard Nixon. They were having a Pepsi-Cola board of directors meeting.[5] She was on the board of Pepsi-Cola and he was the attorney for Pepsi-Cola. So they came to the show, and I'll never forget this was the day before—this was Thursday night—and Clarey introduced her and gave her a very nice introduction, and then when he got to Nixon he said, "And also in the audience is a man—I didn't vote for him." And it was really embarrassing whether you liked Nixon or you didn't like Nixon, it was just a terrible way to make an introduction. Very unprofessional. And he gave him this left-hand introduction, and Nixon stood up and grinned to his teeth and sat down. He left early the next morning. I wrote in my column that I thought it was a very unprofessional

---

[5] The board meeting was held in Dallas.

introduction. Our final panelist—all I can say is he knows more about this thing than any man in the planet. The most respected newsman out of this whole thing, and if he tells you something, you can go to the bank on it because it's true. Hugh Aynesworth.

Aynesworth: Thank you, Tony. I'll be very brief. I just have a couple of stories. Most of you that knew Jack knew a different Jack Ruby than I knew. I did not like Jack Ruby and I'll tell you very briefly why. Besides the Sovereign Club and the Carousel he had a club out on Oak Lawn, an after-hours club. And often I would find myself—I was single in most of the early 60s—and I would find myself out there because in those days it was a brown bottle—brown-bag days, you had to buy a bottle, take it in, drink it all, whatever. And out there, they served only near-beer, so you could go out there, you didn't have to have the bottle with you and all. And every once in a while somebody would sneak a bottle in there.

And I saw Jack one night—he used to come out there after his club closed a lot. His sister Eva actually ran it. And I saw this drunk—and he was obviously drunk—they took his money, cover charge and he had a rather tight suit on anyway, and I saw something sticking out there. I figured it was his bottle. And they took his money, brought him in, and then Jack Ruby pushed him up against the wall and took a billy stick and broke that bottle in his pocket. That was the first time that I saw Jack do something rather—he was a bully, he was a show-off and he was a bully. I got to know the family. I never liked Jack, but I did get to respect the family, who, my god, you can only imagine what the family went through. Eva was sort of a strange lady, but the other brothers and sisters, I got to know them pretty well.

January '67 I had just joined *Newsweek* magazine, and the next day Jack Ruby died. So I ran like the devil when I heard about it to the hospital. And as I'm running up to the hospital, here comes Eva, brother Earl and the other sister from Chicago. I forget her name. And they said, "Come on and go with us." I had gotten to know them during the trial, and I said, "Where arc you going?" And they said to the funeral home.

So I went to the funeral home with the three, the brothers and sisters, and helped them plan the funeral because they were distraught, they didn't know what his birthday was, they didn't know what kind of Veterans' benefits he had, they didn't know how to ship the body back and forth, and so there I was, I went out on Live Oak to the funeral home and helped them essentially plan the funeral, make a couple of phone calls and everything else, and it was really an interesting thing.

There were several really angry reporters and photographers that had followed them and they wouldn't let them in. And I remember, that's probably when I made my first enemies because they were saying, "Aynesworth's in there, why can't I get in there?" And they were clawing the windows and doors. And I remember Shelly Katz particularly. But he does that all the time, I think.

But anyway, as a result of this, the family invited me to be the only newsman inside the closed funeral in Chicago. And of course I had just joined *Newsweek* as I said the day before he died, and so *Newsweek* was very very glad to have me do that. So I went up there and they had the house of shiva. We went to the family's house of course and it was a sad occasion. There were bomb threats and all kinds of strange things that went on, but I already knew and I already had felt in those days preceding—the two years, three years preceding—that there conspiracy people out there who were making up stories, who would do anything to get a story, and I figured if indeed Jack Ruby is buried without somebody looking at him that they're going to dig him up someday or they're going to put pressure and say that's not really Jack Ruby that died. Already I figured they'd do it to Oswald, but it didn't happen until a long time later, so I talked to the family that day, I talked to Earl in particular and Eva and I said you've got to let someone in the press just before you close the casket to examine that body.

Well, they kicked it around for an hour or two and they didn't want to really do it, but they did. Two Chicago newsman and a CBS newsman—I think Nelson Benton—were allowed in at the very last right before they closed the funeral. So maybe we won't have another, somebody coming from Europe and insisting it's not Jack Ruby.

I might tell you one other story that was told to me by a guy named Bob Larkin who was a bouncer for the competitor, Abe, down the street. Later ran a nightclub here in town.[6] Tony knows him, I'm sure. One time, as a bouncer for Abe he got into a fight with a guy and the guy stabbed him. And he was down at the bottom on the street, on Commerce Street. Bob's telling me this. This happened in '61 or so. And he said he is laying there bleeding, the guy ran off, and nobody else is there, he's on the street bleeding and hollering and here comes Jack Ruby walking out of the building, and he says, "What happened? What happened?" And he said, "The guy stabbed me," Bob said. And he [Ruby] said, "Get up, get up," and he kept kicking Larkin. But Ruby was a strange man. But that's about all I have.

Zoppi: I'm going to tell you one final story that'll wrap this up. Earl Ruby and I became very friendly. Earl was his brother and put up the money for the trial and everything, and after it was all over, in fact just a few years ago, he told me, he said the day before Jack died, Earl and his attorney, a fellow named Addelson, went into his hospital room and Earl was carrying a briefcase which was really a tape recorder, and so when they went in Addelson kept the guard occupied talking to the guard. And Earl said he went over to the bed where Jack was and he said, "This is not a tape recorder"—I mean, "This is not a brief case, this is a tape recorder—if you have anything to say, we both know you're a dying man." He said, "Now is the time to say it. So, please, Jack, anything."

And Jack said, "If I hadn't made the U-turn on Main Street that morning none of this would have happened." As you remember, there was a parking lot across from the telegraph office, Western Union, and there wasn't much traffic on Main

---

[6]Abe Weinstein, owner of Colony Club.

Street that Sunday morning, so instead of going up Main Street a couple more blocks, taking another one-way street north, another one-way street west, and then a one-way street south to get into the parking lot, he just made a quick U-turn into the parking lot and saved about four minutes. And that was the difference.

Pappas: I'm looking at this whole thing from the outsider's point of view. You knew Jack, I mean most of you knew Jack Ruby, and I guess we all learned about Oswald at the same time. But thirty years now I've stood firmly on the side of the non-conspirators. I mean I know what the facts are and my overview and I've said this over and over again and I've been attacked at audiences. I've had conspiracy groups assault me, and I said the Warren Commission is right, there was no second shooter, and I'm going to stay with that, and I feel very vindicated now that the temper is changing—the temperament of the story is changing and coming around to that view and reinforcing what we already know.

As far as I'm concerned, and as far as I can read it so far, Oswald was the lone shooter, but the more—over the years I've learned more and more perhaps about a motive—and I do believe that there is a Cuba connection. Precisely what it is I can't say, because I didn't cover that end of it and I haven't really investigated it. But I think there is a possibility that Oswald with his Cuba connections, and his Communist connections and so forth, was acting on behalf of Castro, although I can't prove it. That's the most logical thing for me to try to believe, that Oswald—if there is a motive other than just his displeasure with the United States, and that he was striking out at a symbol of the United States—that if there is any kind of conspiracy it would be that connection.

As far as I'm concerned, and I did not know Ruby before those two instances that I described, he was simply a little guy in a major powerful city who was trying to make a name for himself and who thought that he might serve a couple of years, become a big man, and live happily ever after as a hero in the United States. That was my feeling then, and that is my feeling now. It's nothing more than that. Thank you.

Payne: I want to thank this panel. It has been very good, very informative. Now, hold on one second. I want to apologize for the fact that we haven't had time for questions. We've had just a few questions. There's one question here, though, directed to Hugh, and I know he'll be brief so we can get with our break and start the other. What book, in your opinion, has the most factual coverage of the assassination and other events of the weekend? And then, the second part— what is your opinion of *Case Closed*?

Aynesworth: The best book was probably Jim Bishop's[7] because he didn't get into any conspiratorial situation. Once you throw a hundred different conspiracies out, that becomes a very complex thing. And there is no book that has done the whole thing. There is no market for it, been no market for it. Now *Case Closed* has come along and is making, is swerving public opinion, I think, and you can tell this by the ferocity with which it is being attacked by all these conspiracy theorists. I don't agree with all of it. I was asked to read it by *U.S. News & World Report* before they bought it, but it is a good book, it is an honest book, and I agree with 95 percent of it.

Payne: Thanks, Hugh. We'll take our break now and resume here at about 3:35.

---

[7] *The Day Kennedy Was Shot.* New York: Funk & Wagnalls, 1968.

SIDEBARS

EDDIE BARKER, Moderator

This closing session was devoted to miscellaneous questions and comments, including discussion about the burial of Lee Harvey Oswald and the fact that members of the media were pressed into service as his pallbearers. (This session began at 3:30 p.m. and ended at 4:30 p.m.)

Barker: OK, we call this final panel, we call this final panel our sidebars of the day, and we're going to be talking about some of the things that probably never made the papers and never made radio and television and probably not been told except for a few times when some of us have gotten together and, under the influence of John Barleycorn or something, they really come out. But today, we're baring all, as they say, and we will be on our way. We have several questions here, and if any of you have a question you'd like to write it out bring it up here and we'll see if we can't get it answered.

Now I had one lady ask me awhile ago, and some of you guys would know, what ever happened to Connally's hat? That he was wearing in the limo.[1] She says it has disappeared. Does anybody know? [no response from the audience]

---

[1] Unlike the president, who as was his custom was hatless that day, Texas Governor John B. Connally wore a light-colored Stetson which at the time

Well, that takes care of that.

What happened to the hat Raymond Buck[2] gave the president? Well, it's probably in the Kennedy Library, I would guess. Come up to the mike, Bo [Byers], and tell us.

Byers: I'm not sure, but it [Connally's hat] might be in the State Archives. I know that the suit he was wearing that day is in the Archives. The reason I know that is that I asked him later if he still had a copy of the story I handed him about our [Houston] *Chronicle* poll. He said yes, he said that when Kennedy asked him about it he said he had it in my coat pocket and I didn't show it to him. I said is it still in your coat pocket? He said I don't know. The suit is in the State Archives. We called the State Archives and asked them about it, and they said that suit was sent twice to Washington for examination and that that story would not be there. We're now checking with the Archives at the LBJ Library. Now there are about 50 boxes, if people are interested in that sort of thing, there are about 50 boxes of the Connally papers, and they said we haven't catalogued all of those yet, so we don't know. We might find your story there.

Barker: OK, Thank you very much, Bo. I'm going to quickly run through a couple of these questions, and then we're going to talk about some of the more bizarre things in the coverage of this story. What happened to the minister who reported DISD[3] students in his church were cheering about the assassination? Actually, he was talking about the University Park School over here in the Highland Park system. Someone told me recently I think he now has a church in Washington, in Washington, D.C. That's right.

---

the shots were fired he was holding in his right hand as he sat in the front seat of the presidential limousine.

[2]Buck was president of the Fort Worth Chamber of Commerce. He presented a western hat to President Kennedy (which the president declined to put on) in the morning ceremony at the Texas Hotel in Fort Worth before the entourage left for Dallas.

[3]Dallas Independent School District.

And here is another one. At least two reporters have mentioned seeing Tippit's casket or possibly Tippit's body at Parkland. I understood Tippit was DOA at Methodist. Can someone clarify this? Who'd like to take that on? Come up here, Jerry, to the mike. You qualify as—this is Jerry Hill, who had a career with Channel 5 [then WBAP-TV, later KXAS-TV] and then with the *Times Herald* and Channel 4 [then KRLD-TV, later KDFW-TV], that's right, and also with the Dallas PD [Police Department].[4] And Jerry had an awful lot to do with an awful lot of things. So straighten us up.

Hill: He was taken to Methodist Central, which is on Colorado [Boulevard], by Dudley Hughes Ambulance. But when they wanted a post-mortem, for legal purposes the medical examiner was at Parkland, so they transferred the body over there for the post-mortem. That's how the body got to Parkland.

Barker: OK, thank you, Jerry. Why is there no copy of the full-page ad denouncing JFK on display here?[5] Frankly, we didn't have one, we certainly were not trying to suppress it, but our archival, our archivist just didn't have the copy of it. What happened to Tippit's widow? And the $600,000 that the American public contributed to her? Jerry, you might be in a position I guess as much as anyone else to respond to that. What was the amount of money that Mrs. Tippit got? Mike, you followed that.

Mike Cochran:[6] The last I heard was $600,000.

---

[4]Gerald Lynn Hill not only was one of the first police officers to enter and search the Texas School Book Depository, he also was one of the first to arrive at the site of the J.D. Tippit shooting in Oak Cliff at 10th and Patton streets. Minutes later he and several officers arrested Oswald at the Texas Theater on Jefferson Boulevard.

[5]A reference to the black-bordered advertisement which appeared in the *Dallas Morning News* on the morning of the assassination which contained scurrilous charges that the president was a dupe of communism.

[6]Fort Worth-based correspondent for Associated Press.

Barker: How about $600,000?

Hill: It was about $600,000.[7] What happened was that she asked some specific police officers. Glen King, who was later chief of police, was one of them. V.K. Hipskind, who was another. They counted all the money. They were the ones that made the deposits. They counseled her on getting an investment counselor. Trust funds were set up for her and the kids. She later married another police officer who has since died, and she is a widow and is still fairly active, I understand, in the Police Officers' Wives organization.

Barker: OK, Thank you, Jerry again.

Milligan: Excuse me, Eddie, I think I can answer why that ad's not up here.

Barker: What? What, who's not up here?

Milligan: The ad, or the letter, in the *Dallas News*.

Barker: Yeah, go ahead.

Milligan: I don't believe there was a much coordinated effort. I'm not faulting Darwin Payne or anybody. It was up to the media to bring displays up there.

Barker: No, we were not trying to get displays. We actually want to thank our historian, Ferris Ruckstool, who supplied us with most of these, and he is the one responsible for bringing the things that we have, and we do appreciate

---

[7] Slain police officer J.D. Tippit's widow, Marie, received substantial donations from benefactors from throughout the country after her husband's death. She put half the money in trust for her children. In 1967 the amount she had received was reported by William Manchester to be $643,863. Marina Oswald also received similar donations, but far less, approximately $70,000.

that very much, Ferris. A couple of other questions. With all the hours Oswald spent being interrogated, why was there apparently no record, no tape, written or otherwise of the responses, from the most notorious criminal suspect of the century? OK, and I know several of you want to get on that. Mike, do you want to try it?

Cochran: I wasn't involved with that part of it. No, I really wasn't.

Barker: OK, Wes, come on up here to the mike and tell us about—what you know about that. I've heard a version of it, let's see if it's the same one.

Wise: In the oral histories that Bob Porter and I are doing for the Dallas County Historical Foundation, Henry Wade made the statement there was no tape recorder in the police station. Nor was there any at the Dallas County headquarters. You've got to remember, tape recording was just coming in, it was just getting popular at that time, and to have that kind of equipment at that time was fairly far advanced.[8] Now that was just Henry's statement.

Barker: OK, thank you. I had always heard that story, and I know Tim Timmons was in the audience earlier today, who was the assistant U.S. d[istrict]. a[ttorney]. at the time, and Bob Gemberling from the FBI was here, and I had always heard the story that Captain Fritz just kind of took charge of that interrogation and he just didn't want any help from anybody, and he asked the questions. And that's probably about as close to being right as you can be. And, Captain ran his own ship, and it was not a federal offense. Isn't that correct, at the time? It was a state case and it was handled by the Dallas Police Department. OK, come on up, Jim.

---

[8]Not really. Tape recorders found limited use in Britain and Germany in the 1930s, and they came into wide use in the United States after World War II.

Ewell: The investigation of the president's murder was a state offense. It was not covered by federal statutes at that time. Now, I understand that Congress had written laws protecting all the other government officials, but for some reason the president was omitted. Now, Tim Timmins, is that correct? OK, so it was a state offense. The FBI was simply assisting the Dallas Police Department in the investigation. That's all they could do. It did not cover federal jurisdiction.

Barker: OK, now here's one [a written question from the audience]. I don't really understand. But maybe together we can figure this out, huh? "I have really enjoyed hearing these journalists recalling that weekend. For the most part, it sounds as if a good job was done. That being the case, how did the ball get dropped so badly so shortly thereafter?" I don't understand the question, so we can't answer that. Something that I've always wondered about, Mike Cochran. You were over at the Cellar,[9] were you not?

Cochran: I was with the Secret Service and the White House staff and all that crew Thursday night before the assassination. They went to—everybody was at the Press Club [of Fort Worth], and the reason for that was back then of course there was no place in town to get a mixed drink. We didn't have liquor-by-the-drink back in the stone age, and so everybody came to the Press Club. And about 3 o'clock I think some of the Secret Service agents and some other folks just headed to the Cellar, and I think they had a Senate inquiry into the Cellar, and the Secret Service some time after that. But I didn't—I had to be up the next morning, so I didn't get to go to the Cellar.

Cochran

Barker: I'm going to ask something personal now. This is kind of an inside thing, and unless you know Huffaker and

---

[9] A late-night bar/coffee shop noted as a Fort Worth "Beatnik" hangout.

Wise and all of this group of mine back in those days you won't really appreciate this, but you'll bear with me. Bob was down in the basement that morning and he and Nelson Benton, the late Nelson Benton, were kind of taking turns just sort of waiting things out until they brought Lee Oswald out. So when they brought him down it turned out that Bob [Huffaker] had the mike, and I was back in the newsroom, and we were all watching this, and Bob starts screaming into the mike, "Lee Harold has been shot. Lee Harold has been shot." And I'm kicking the wastebasket and saying, "His name ain't Harold." And Huffaker has got—can tell us why he called him Lee Harold, and he's going to hang it on somebody we all know.

Huffaker: They're going to put that on my epitaph. My Andy Warhol fifteen minutes.

Barker: Don't take fifteen minutes to tell this, please.

Huffaker: What happened was when Nelson [Benton] and Dan Rather and I were sort of rotating around city hall and trading off with the CBS live television mike, one of us would stand by the mike and New York would call for us on just a couple of minutes notice and we would have to give a summary of how everything stood at that time. And also, we would be among those pushy television reporters who would crowd up to Chief Curry and the other officials who passed through the hallways up there. And Dan spent most of his time elsewhere in town, but Nelson and I would circulate around the police station and try to verify items of information and do that sort of thing.

And during one of those times on the Saturday before Oswald was shot on Sunday, I thought, well—I had gone by the way—I had been at Parkland Hospital the previous evening and my assignment at the police station didn't begin until that Saturday [Sunday] morning, so I had a full set of notes that I had already received from Warren Fulkes who had been our reporter there the previous night, and on that set of notes it had all the correct information. It had "Lee Harvey Oswald, age 24, ex-Marine," and all of those items that I needed to know to go ahead and continue the reporting.

And I thought, well, nobody has really gone in and checked the public information officer yet, so during a time when Nelson had the mike I left and went down to Glen King's office. He was the police public information officer at the time, and Glen King, wherever you are, I'm going to blame you for this. But I sat down across the desk from Glen and I began to go through my notes and just double-check every piece of information I had because I was always very thorough. Later became a college professor, you can understand. So I went over every item of information. "Lee Harvey Oswald," I read him, and he said, "No, it's Lee Harold Oswald." And I said, "Well, now, everybody has been, since yesterday everybody has been saying, 'Lee Harvey Oswald.' Are you certain that this is Lee Harold Oswald?" And he said, "Absolutely, it's Lee Harold Oswald." And I said, "Well, now, Glen, where did you get that information?" And he said, "I got it off the arrest record."

So I thought OK. And I marked it out. I still have my notes where I marked out "Lee Harvey," and wrote in "Lee Harold." And from that moment on I thought I was the only guy who was right. I had ruined myself for history.

Barker: OK, thank you, Bob. Here is something for Jack Tinsley. Jack, someone wants to know, how did you manage to get in the School Book Depository Building after the drive over from Fort Worth since it was closed off immediately after the assassination. Making his way now to the mike is Mr. Tinsley, who moved a little faster when he came into—

Tinsley: Well, the answer is, I don't know. But I got in. I hitchhiked from Parkland Hospital downtown. I got in and the foreman took me up to the sixth floor. I don't know what time it was. I wasn't keeping track of the time. But I did get in. It was not closed off. And I was there.[10]

---

[10]A number of journalists were permitted inside the Depository in the

Barker: OK. I don't know how many of you remember that this really was the second visit of JFK to Dallas during his presidency. And the first visit—and a lot of us in this room covered that—he came to say a deathbed goodbye to Sam Rayburn. And I remember we were all out at Baylor Hospital and I was out there—I had been out there a good bit over the last month since two of our daughters had presented us with new grandchildren in that time, and the other thing when I was up there and thinking about coming to this meeting today, and I remembered back, and sure enough the president was out there, and he was in and out of town and nothing like this took place.

Milligan: He went to Mr. Sam's funeral[11] in Bonham, Texas, and his picture is in the darned Press Club office, and can I add a comment to what was asked about why the ball was dropped? That is presuming and assuming that this conspiracy, etc., etc.—I agree with Mary Woodward this morning. That's my personal opinion. I don't know. But keep in mind early in the sixties, print media was dominant; television and the electronic is dominant now. But I want to correct something about the Secret Service men didn't pin me and Bill Winfrey to the—our memory is getting a little fuzzy about it, but a rookie cop tried to pull a gun on us. But I made two whiskey runs and that was mentioned, and I didn't find any whiskey for Baskin. I found Coca-Cola up Harry Hines Boulevard, and Paul Crume didn't touch a pint of whiskey but Krueger sent me over to the old Dallas Hotel to get him a pint and I carried it in and set it on the desk and he said, "Thanks, Tom." Some of this anti-Dallas business—

Barker: Sam, er,—Tom, we really would like to—I don't want to cut you short, but we do want to kind of keep this thing moving along. Here's a question. "Who were the

---

afternoon after police had concluded their preliminary investigation.

[11] Speaker of the House Sam Rayburn died on November 16, 1961.

pallbearers for Oswald's funeral?" Will the pallbearers present please stand? One, two, three, four. I thought we had five. [Voice from crowd: "Jerry Flemmons [*Fort Worth Star-Telegram* reporter] is ill."] Jerry is ill? OK. Who would like to tell the story on that? Mike [Cochran], why don't you? Do you want to tell it or do you want Mike to tell it?

Eddie Hughes: I do want to say one thing about it. Of course, the big issue on that day was whether or not Oswald's body was actually in the coffin. And the police chief finally— he didn't want to be fooled either, and he went to check it. But, when it came time to taking the casket down the biggest issue was who was going to carry it down? There weren't any

Hughes

family members whatever. And so I finally ended up on one of the corners, and the thing that scared the living daylights out of me was —two things, one, that sucker was heavy, and—I had never lifted a casket in my life; I didn't realize they were heavy, particularly with bodies in there. And number two, I represented the *Dallas Morning News,* a very conservative newspaper, and here I was carrying the assassin down to the grave site. Thank God somebody said this is making history, and since I also had to shoot photographs I popped off and the fellow—both of the guys replaced me on the casket, and I got these fellows carrying it down to the grave site.

Barker: Well, now, I heard this story, and Mac [Preston McGraw] you and Cochran will have to get me straight on this. One of you started out to be a pallbearer and the other said, "Well, if the AP is there I got to be there too," or, "If the UPI is there I got to be there too." What's the story?

Cochran: Just the opposite. They were recruiting, but number one, everyone has got to understand that Oswald's popularity that day was at an all-time low. So, there weren't a bunch of people running up to volunteer, and so when they tried to get somebody to do it. Well, two things. It became obvious that if we were going to write a story about the burial of Lee Harvey Oswald we were going to have to bury him ourselves. So, then they—what they did was to say—I don't remember who it was that asked me to do it, and I said no. And I turned around and there was Preston McGraw of UPI jumping right up there. And I said if UPI is going to do it, I've got to do it. So, Preston who spent a career kicking my ass—I wasn't going to let him do it on the coffin.

Jon McConal: My name is Jon McConal. I work for the *Star-Telegram* still. When I worked for them then I know how our memories change. I knew Drudie Miller, the guy who brought the body out there. I was the night police reporter, and Drudie walked over to me, and he said, "Jon, will you help me unload the body?" And there was absolutely, Mac is right—the only people there was the Oswald family and the preacher. And so Drudie said, "Do you think the newsmen will be pallbearers?" And I said, "Well, I'm sure they will." And Cochran was right, too. And as a result Oswald had one too many pallbearers. You normally have eight, and he had nine around the casket. One other thing, I remember—

McConal

Barker: Well, who was the ninth one, then?

McConal: I do not remember. I know there were two

Barker: Was one of them a Secret Service agent? I've heard that one of them was an agent.

McConal: Well, I know we had one too many.

Barker: All right, we have a dispute here that many never be settled.

McConal: Somebody will write a book about it, I assure you.

Barker: Either there were seven or there were nine.

McConal: The other thing that I remember about all this was there was a reporter there from a paper I will not name, and he immediately—after the casket got there—he started saying that was not a body in there, there was a sack of potatoes in there. And that was a conspiracy theory that already started that they were burying potatoes instead of Oswald.

And one other quick thing about my part in it. When we got back at the *Star-Telegram* we had approximately six people out there. And one of our reporters was a guy who spoke Russian, and he had interviewed Marina. And so "Chief" Craig, the one you met this morning—that huge man, he's about six-foot-five, and I had never seen Chief mad but one time anyway. He came over to me. My nickname is Bunky, and he said, "Bunky, I want you to get the notes from the rest of the reporters, and you write the story." So I started around and all the reporters agreed except Dan—this other reporter— Dan Bates—I'll give his name. And he said since he worked for the afternoon paper he was going to write an exclusive about his interview with Marina. So Dan was quite a big fellow himself, and I learned early on in life that the bigger they are, the harder they fall is not necessarily true. The bigger they are, the harder they knock hell out of you. So I went over and told Chief Craig that everybody had given me their notes but Dan Bates. And Chief Craig went over and he said, "Dan, I want you to give Bunky your notes." And Dan said, "I'm writing this exclusively for the evening *Star-Telegram*." And Chief's nose started getting red and he reached down and grabbed Dan by the shoulder, and he said, "You son of a bitch, you're going to give Bunky your notes." And Dan said, "Yessir, I'm typing them right now." And finally the kicker of it is it was a terrible interview because he had asked her such things as was she really from Russia? And what kind of country was Russia?

Barker: We have—OK, here is another question from that vast audience out there. Incidentally, if you have any more questions, get them up here and we'll try to answer them. You can see how fully we answer these questions. "Please fully explain the dry chicken bones mentioned earlier." I'll take a little bit of a hand at that, and anybody else who wants to join in. Do what? OK, come on up, [Gerald] Hill, and see if your story varies from mine. All right, there were these three guys in the fifth-floor window, James Jarman [Jr.], Bonnie Ray Williams, and Harold Norman, and they had lunch there. Are you going to dispute me?[12]

Gerald Hill:[13] Nope. We had two sets of chicken bones in the School Book Depository. When we went into the building to search it, and we got there before Captain [Will] Fritz did, so we did police procedure. There was an officer named Roy Westphal, there were deputy sheriffs, one of them's name was [Luke] Mooney, I do not remember the other ones' names, myself, and a uniformed officer. We went to the top floor,  which was the seventh floor. We checked the roof, we came back to the seventh floor, we searched it, we left the uniformed officer on the seventh floor so that anybody in the building could not double back on us and get behind us in an area we had already cleared. We went down to the sixth floor and at that point Moody found the barricade that would have sealed off the window from the view of the rest of the sixth floor. We found the boxes that he had used for an arm rest, and on top of this barricade type thing

Hill

---

[12] All three of these men were employees at the Texas School Book Depository.

[13] See footnote on page 135 for Hill's background.

was a paper sack with some chicken bones in it. Now, we found these on the sixth floor.

I went down to the street to get the crime lab. That point is when we met Fritz at the front door. I explained to him what we found. He went in the building. I went out to report to the senior officer at the location. We stopped our investigation when we found the spot where the shots were fired from, and later on the same floor on the sixth floor where the rifle was found. The people talking about getting into the building later when we got all the physical evidence out of there. We got the fingerprints, we got the hulls, we got the rifle, and we had no more use for the Student [School] Book Depository because we couldn't take it to court.

Barker: OK, but straighten—you say the bones, you found them on the sixth. I thought they were on the fifth.

Hill: I never went to the fifth. There could have well been some down there, which I understand there were. I'm not disputing the fact they were on the fifth floor also. But these were not. Didn't play a big part in it, other than that that was the first thing he saw he could take a picture of as he said this morning.

Barker: OK. [Reads a series of questions from the audience.] "Tom Dillard mentioned a flat-bed truck having been removed from the front of the motorcade at the last minute. Does anyone know why the change was made?" Also, "Was the parade route changed at the last minute?" Nope.

Dillard: [inaudible]

Barker: We can't hear you.

Dillard: Can you hear me?

Barker: Yep.

Dillard: I'm not positive that we were actually going to have a flat-bed truck. It was the custom; we expected it; and we were told that we would have one prior to the trip to Love Field. Now, of course I don't know who stopped it. Someone mentioned Lyndon Johnson stopped it. I don't know; does anyone know?

Barker: It was what the cameramen to ride on. Tom, you were in a convertible as I remember. Were you in that convertible with who was in that, Jim Underwood? Which one was he in?

Dillard: Jim Underwood was with me and Bob Jackson. Bob, do you remember who else was there?

Jackson: Malcolm Couch.[14] I think he was in there.

Dillard: I think so. And then of course the driver. Whoever the driver was we don't know. We were—people have told me, the FBI and what-not in the interview, said that we were six in the car in the parade, number six. Is that what you heard, Bob?

Jackson: inaudible.

Barker: Bob, get up to the mike, if you would, thanks.

Jackson: I think we were the eighth car from the very lead car. We might have been six back from the president, but there was a police car and then there was—I think we were eighth.

Dillard: I heard we were sixth from the president.

Jackson: Right, that's probably right.

---

[14]A news cameraman for WFAA-TV.

Dillard: We could have very well been two miles; it made no difference.

Jackson: That's right.

Barker: OK, "Oswald's mother claims her being a single mother and absence—" I didn't realize that term, "single parent," was used thirty years ago. I thought that was a fairly, fairly, fairly, fairly new. "Oswald's mother claims her being a single mother and absence of a father for Oswald for the way Oswald turned out. What can you tell us about Oswald's brother, Robert?" I never knew Robert, but I saw him on "Front Line" the other night, and he looked like a pretty normal, sensible sort of guy. There's not much doubt in his mind that— Jerry come tell us about that. McNeill. Come up. Yeah, Cochran, you know that, go ahead.

McNeill: Lee was raised by his mother; I don't think Bob was. He was off at military school or boarding school or something like that. I had a couple of encounters with Marguerite Oswald, and if you ever had an encounter with Marguerite Oswald you might better understand Lee's psychology. She was something else.

Within a couple of weeks of her son having been accused of committing the assassination of the president and himself being killed we went over to do a TV and word interview, Jack Clingy, a TV guy from UPI Movie-tone News and put the hustle on us from the time we hit the front door. Her first reaction was, well, the lights are— I can't— the electricity, I can hardly pay the bill, and a twenty-dollar bill would help pay her electric bill. It got us inside, and then she was talking about no food in the house and the cameraman got in his car and went down to the Seven-Eleven and bought a sack of groceries and that got us an interview with Marguerite Oswald.

Again, it was something that I don't think was quite normal for a mother who had just lost a son under those circumstances. And then, years later—a year or so later, with the release of the Warren Commission Report, and it was released to the media in Washington about forty-eight hours ahead of—released to the general public and they put a copy of the report on the plane to me here in Dallas and wanted a picture of some of the participants or some of the people involved in the thing, and we chose Marguerite and there was a young reporter whose name I don't remember with the *Fort Worth Press* at that time who was kind of handling her business for her. And we called him. Would she pose with a picture of the book? And he called me back later on and said she would do it for twenty-five dollars. Twenty-five dollars. And I've still got a photocopy of the receipt that I made her give me. "Received of UPI, $25 for posing for the book." She was a nut.

Barker: Well, I'll tell you

McNeill: She was a nut.

Barker: Anybody who ever had any dealings with Marguerite Oswald would amen that she heard a little different drummer.

McNeill: She went to a little different drummer, but Bob in all that I remember and Mike [Cochran] you may know more about this. He was not raised by Marguerite. He was separated.

Cochran: That's right. I really never knew Robert. I met him but I never knew him, but the Secret Service agent, Mike Howard, who was the one with Charley Kunkel who guarded the Oswald family after the from Sunday the Sunday right before Oswald was shot until the following Friday. They said that Robert Oswald was just a really nice guy, very supportive, and totally estranged from Marguerite.

Barker: He sure came across that way in that "Front Line" piece.

Cochran: And they could not say enough nice things about him. But I don't really know him.

Barker: I have one here. "Can any one present address the timing factor involved from when Oswald shot JFK from the sixth floor and when he was spotted in the downstairs break room on the second floor drinking a Coke?"

Milligan: That's in the Warren Commission Report. I don't remember the time,

Barker: That was Officer—that was Baker,[15] I think, wasn't it?

Milligan: Hey, Eddie, do you know what caused the fist fight between Gordon Yoder and Jimmy Breslin at the Press Club on Friday night?

Barker: I have no—I didn't know there was a fight between Gordon Yoder and—

Milligan: Yeah, they did. I went up there on Saturday night and they said you missed a show Friday night. Said Yoder punched Breslin, big New York columnist.

Barker: OK, here's a question. "Will videotape of the conference be available?" I thought you'd never ask. "If so, what will be the cost?" You shouldn't have asked. "And who can you order it from?" We are taping this. SMU is taping the whole thing. CSPAN is of course taping it, and I understand. We may get a schedule from CSPAN before we leave today as

---

[15] Dallas motorcycle police officer Marrion Baker, riding in the presidential motorcade, was the first officer to get inside the Texas School Book Depository Building. He began searching the building with manager Roy Truly within a few moments of the shooting. When they encountered Oswald on the second floor Baker asked Truly if he knew him. Truly identified him as an employee and Baker continued his search without stopping or questioning Oswald..

to when they'll be playing it back? And do you want to—why don't you, if you will, Darwin, explain about it.

Payne: The videotape, of course is being done today, and we intend as soon as possible to start editing that into a one-hour tape, perhaps an hour-and-a-half—it seems so good—and if you're interested in that stay in touch with the Center for Communication Arts, SMU.   Center for Communication Arts. Telephone number is 768-3028.

Barker: That's your number.

Payne: That's my number. I can't remember the number for us. What is it, Laura Hlavach?   768-3090. I know that's right. And also the photograph.

Barker: And also, are you not planning on doing the verbatim proceedings of this?

Payne: Perhaps. Perhaps a verbatim proceeding. We'll see how it looks and try to put it together in a pamphlet form.

From the audience: Sound tape?

Payne: Sound tape. You're the second person who has asked about that. We hadn't thought about it to start with, but it looks like there is a market out there for a sound tape.

Barker: We just may just sell tapes all—we didn't know existed.

Payne: Finally, the photograph. The group photograph that was taken by Farris Ruckstool will be available as well from the Center for Communication Arts, SMU, 768-3090. And we'll talk to Farris about reproducing those photos. That can be ordered as well, and I have no idea what the appropriate price would be.

Barker: OK, next question. "How quickly was the Zapruder film released to the press? Did Zapruder make the film available, did he present it to the government, etc?" I want to say that there is a lady here, Bobbie—and I'm sorry, Bobbie, I don't remember your last name[16]—and I was on a talk show the other night promoting this event and she called and she was the lady out at Kodak who processed that film that day. We're delighted, Bobbie, that you're with us today. She told me that the FBI—I think I'm right on this story—see if I remember things correctly. That the FBI brought that film in, said they wanted it run then, shut down the plant and do it. Plant manager said I can't do that until I call Rochester. He called Rochester and they did the film. They shut it down.

Milligan: Harry McCormick came up to the *Dallas News*, Eddie, and said that he could buy it for something like ten or twelve grand and they said no.

Barker: Let's talk to people who were actually negotiating for it. And I think you were. Yeah, come on Tom [Dillard]. Why don't you—and I think Darwin Payne also was involved in that, too. Go ahead.

Dillard: I took Harry out there that night as they were processing the film. I was trying to get Zapruder to allow me to make a copy of one of his frames for us to run in the morning paper showing the car with people in it. At the same time I think I had, as I remember, I may be wrong, I think I had permission to offer about $50, as I remember it—this could be wrong—for Mr. Zapruder's permission. But I know my pitch was that if you'll let me have this and we put it in the *Dallas News* this one picture will be great publicity for your film, which should bring you more profit for it. Which seemed to me a pretty good pitch. But Harry's profit, God rest his crazy soul, was to get control of it so he could be cut in on the profit which Harry immediately foresaw as a rather large amount as it turned out.

---

[16]Hicks.

Barker: The bidding, I think, that I heard the story, got up from I think some people were offering as much as $1,500, $1,700 for that. And what was the final price that Time-Life paid? I heard $250,000. Was that pretty much it? OK. "Why doesn't someone talk about Jack Krueger, editor of the *Dallas Morning News*, on the grand jury and the judge wouldn't excuse him." Whoever wrote that question probably wasn't here this morning because we went into great detail on that.

Milligan: Well, he came in mad as hell and he—

Barker: OK, "Bill Payette was head of UPI;[17] his wife Ginnie [Virginia] was called from the bridge table to go to Parkland. She held the phone until Merriman Smith arrived." Well, I didn't know that. OK, let's see. Where do we go from here? We had some—"How did Eddie Barker get the TV interview with Marina Oswald?" Connections.

Huffaker: Eddie, did it have anything to do with Heinekin's Beer?

Barker: Heineken's? With Marina?

Huffaker: Didn't you buy Marina Oswald some Heineken Beer?

Barker: No, she, no, no, no, no.

Huffaker: Is that another conspiracy?

Barker: Kahlua. It was Kahlua.

Huffaker: OK.

---

[17]Payette was Southwest regional manager for United Press International.

Barker: The—well, this is—is this the day to confess? OK, "How many witnesses were present at the theater when Lee Harold—Lee Harvey—was arrested? And why have so few of them ever been interviewed?" Well, I think they've all been interviewed. I know McDonald[18] was interviewed. Jerry—this man was everywhere. He was on the magic carpet that day. Get around to the mike.

Hill: One of the main reasons that some of the witnesses at the theater were never interviewed were that they were hookey shooters, and when we went in the front door they went out the back. The second thing was, there were seven officers actually in on the arrest. And that included McDonald, C.T. Walker, Ray Hawkins, Tommy Hudson, Bob Carroll, K.E. Lines, Paul Bentley and myself. In addition to that, there were several other officers inside the theater and outside the theater, but there were very, very few patrons in the theater at that time of the afternoon anyway. And as far as I know, at one time or another, probably every, all policemen had been talked to, and probably all of the customers who weren't hookey shooters have been talked to.

Barker: You talking about the kids upstairs in the balcony? Should have been in class. OK, "Would you comment on the relationship between the local reporters and national reporters. . ." I think we've been commenting on that all day ". . . as it relates to coverage of events of the assassination. I think we've pretty well covered that. "I would like to hear more information—I would like to have more information—on the tone of the setting in Dallas prior to the president's visit. Details, please." Well, again, I think we've pretty well covered that. We had the—I'll tell you a story. Wes, come up. You— here's the guy who—he will not be remembered for his great days as the moderator on "Swap and Shop," that great

---

[18]Dallas police officer M.N. McDonald was the officer closest to Oswald when he was arrested in the Texas Theater. Oswald hit him in the face and attempted to fire his pistol, but McDonald deflected the hammer with his hand and prevented the weapon from firing.

garbage sale of the air we used to do or the fact that he was mayor of Dallas, but he will be remembered because he took the film of that lady with that stick hitting Adlai Stevenson over the head. And why don't you—and there's also sort of a follow-up to that that you might want to get into.

Wise: Well, Jim Underwood and I were at the theater—the Memorial Auditorium Theater—where the U.N. Day was being observed. And by the way, I don't remember anybody remembers this or not. Jim would remember it if he were here today, if he were still alive, but there's a riser on that stage that was up about that far. The riser had not been lowered completely. And after the voices of the National Indignation Society [Committee] and the other demonstrators with their banners and so forth really got ugly. For some reason, don't ask me why, that riser went—upppphh—and fell down level with the stage, and I thought Adlai Stevenson's eyes were going to pop right out. Scared the devil out of him, and it scared Jim Underwood and me, too.

Anyway, it got to be about 9:40 and Jim and I were conversing back and forth and we said, "Look, we can't leave now. It's too electric in here. Something could happen." By that time all the other television reporters had left. I think there was one still photographer from UPI or somewhere I think was still there. Jerry, was it you, Jerry [McNeill]? Well, all the TV reporters were gone, and Jim had the weather to do at 10:15 and I had the sports to do at 10:22, and so I got the job of staying on because my sportscast was seven minutes later than his weathercast.

So, I followed Stevenson out the door, and they were roping out behind—they had some ropes that people there were—Vallian and—I'm sorry, I can't remember your name— Murray were standing there and Adlai Stevenson, who was then ambassador to the U.N. went over to speak to them and this lady came from behind and struck him rather hard over the ear as you can see in those films here and down at the Eighth Floor—Sixth Floor exhibit. I've always suspected that my news director put Walter Cronkite up to it, but he put the film on that night on the 6 o'clock news, ran it back and ran it back twice and said I want to thank that young, alert cameraman in Dallas, Texas, Wes Wise for that great film. Did you put him up to that?

Barker: I did indeed.

Wise: After that, I think this is very important.

Barker: I was just trying to help you along, Wes.

Wise: Yeah, that really helped. I got a $50 check from CBS. Later on, this is pretty important because the Secret Service and FBI were blamed along with the Dallas police for lack of preparation. I went over that Adlai Stevenson film frame by frame with our friends of the Secret Service and the FBI and I think part of our ulterior motive was to get on their good side. But we looked and examined very closely the people in the background of the Adlai Stevenson film for fear that they might be present at the Trade Mart. As a consequence I was not only assigned to the Trade Mart to cover it by Eddie, but also assigned by the Secret Service and FBI if I saw any of these characters that we observed in the frames of the Adlai Stevenson film that I was to notify or to stop one of the Secret Service men or the FBI.

So, if you hear that the FBI and Secret Service weren't doing a lot of work in preparation, that's not quite so because we went over that thing three or four days as I recall. And tried to pick out people who might be suspicious.

Barker: You know, that—you started to get into something that—we used to do in those days, and today we'd all be drummed out of the corps, but we thought that the police were pretty nice people and they thought that we were pretty nice people, and we used to do a lot of back-scratching and it helped us along the way, and we think, or I think that we helped them along the way, but as I say in today's society or in today's media that would be a no-no and we'd probably be out there selling shoes somewhere. OK, next question: "Was

Oswald walking toward Jack Ruby's apartment?"— this always comes up—"at 12th and Marsalis when he shot Officer Tippit and the corner block of East 10th."[19] He was right out there in that area. Who wants to take that on? I've been out there and seen that and sure enough he was kind of right.

Warren G. Harding: [from his seat in the audience, largely inaudible, but a general description of the neighborhood and an affirmation of the fact that Oswald was heading generally toward the area of Ruby's apartment.

Barker: OK, thank you, Warren. That's Warren Harding. That's not the former president Warren Harding,[20] but the former state treasurer Warren Harding. Thank you, Warren, I appreciate that. There's no doubt about it, he was out there in the same neighborhood. "Do you think the country has finally—quote 'forgiven'—unquote, Dallas?" I've had a couple of—well, we could kick this around a while, but I've got two theories as to what really—well, three theories, I guess, and see if you agree with me. One is that—one of the things that really helped Dallas as much as anything else were the Dallas Cowboys. The second thing was the TV show, "Dallas." And I swear I can't remember what the third thing was. What? Oh, the cheerleaders, that's right. Anything—Bob, did you want to add anything to that?

Huffaker: Yeah, I wanted to say, and Wes Wise being mayor for seven years.

Barker: Ah, yes, OK. "Who put. . . ?" [Barker interrupts himself as he before he can finish the question.] You know, there were a couple of people that I did want to get to before

---

[19]Ruby's apartment was at S. Ewing Street and East R.L. Thornton Freeway. Officer Tippit was shot at the corner of 10th and Patton streets.

[20]Harding was Dallas County treasurer in 1963. He later became state treasurer.

we get too far down the road. One was John De La Garza. John, are you here? Come up to the mike. It's a kind of interesting story here. John was a student then. You can see that he has not aged as much as the rest of us, and—ah, that's right, he was a mere child. John was a student out at the University of Texas in Austin, and he was on the *Daily Texan* down there, and a bunch of those enterprising types got on a chartered airplane and came up here to cover it. Right?

De La Garza: Yeah, back then we thought, as probably the folks on the *Texan* staff do now, that we were the best daily in Austin. Probably still are. Thank you. Although we published only five days a week and I guess that's the same, we didn't publish on Saturday or Monday. But what happened was most of us heard it one way or the other on Friday afternoon right after lunch. And most of us went straight to the Journalism Building, the old J-School, which is now the Geography Building, where my son studies, and we hovered around the AP wire. Dave McNeely was the editor and our managing editor was Richard Cole, who is now the dean of the J-School at UNC-Chapel Hill. News editor was Charmayne Marsh who was supposed to be here to do this today, but she used to be on Jim Wright's staff and now works in Washington.

De La Garza

And we, a bunch of us huddled—I was very junior staff then—and we decided—they decided—we needed to publish an extra on Saturday, but to do that we needed to get people to Dallas. So three—Charmayne, the news editor; Richard Cole, the managing editor; and Jim Seymour, an extraordinarily talented photographer and a very large man at the time—got in a little, fairly small single-engine aircraft I think the Longhorn Flying Club chartered from them—and came on up here. Three of us drove. They did their thing a lot earlier than we did wherever they could at Parkland and the School Book Depository.

We hit up here somewhere around six that evening finally in a car, 5:30 or 6; rendezvoused with them and spent the rest of the evening in the city hall on the third floor. An incredible atmosphere, as everybody has talked about. The streets were eerily quiet, I remember I think. Was that the old Topper? That little diner across the street. Topper? Now a parking garage. We ate there that time.

Barker: Everything in downtown Dallas, John, is a parking garage. Thank you, thank you. Or parking lot.

De La Garza: But we did our thing. Jim Seymour kept running out of film, and the word spread that there was a college team there. He never lacked for film. Once that was understood, everybody was our friend, everybody liked the fact that there was a college team there, and we really didn't know what the hell we were doing but we thought we did. My goal, as the most junior member of the staff, and my job as the Catholic in the crowd was to find the priest who had given the president the last rites, so I hit a pay phone some place out on the streets and we started calling and finally tracked down the Rev. Oscar Huber, who is now dead, who was the pastor at Holy Trinity Church. Six years later that became my parish church and remains so. So it's kind of strange how life, how life goes on.

Barker: Thank you very much, John, for sharing that with us. And speaking of—someone asked earlier about that ad, the "Thank You, Mr. President." And John Weeks, who was one of the editorial writers at the *Times Herald* at the time, and I were talking earlier and he said, "You know, it's kind of an interesting headline they had on that ad because they stole it from you." Right, John?

Weeks: Well, you heard about two statements, "Welcome Mr. President," the one back here was the *Star-Telegram,* and of course the headline of the scurrilous ad in the *Dallas News.* Well, there was a third one. On Thursday evening, the day before the president's arrival, our lead editorial in the *Herald* said, "Welcome, Mr. President." And it was a sincere editorial by A.C. Greene.

At the time of the assassination A.C. Greene and I were on  the editorial page staff. Actually, we just weren't on the editorial page staff, hell, we were the editorial page staff. As has been pointed out earlier, overstaffing was never a fault of the *Dallas Times Herald*. But, at any rate, this editorial ran the evening before, and there were a couple of lines at the end I might quickly read to you. The next-to-the-last paragraph, which I now wish that had been the last, says "The eyes of the world also follow the president of the United States at home, or abroad. The eyes of the world are following him to Dallas." We should have quit there.

Weeks

Barker: Quit while you're ahead.

Weeks: And the last line says, unfortunately, "We believe both the world and John F. Kennedy will like what is seen here."

Barker: OK, John, thanks for sharing that with us. We're going to wrap this up here in a minute because it is going to be supper time somewhere before too long, but here's a question that I was discussing with someone over here during one of the breaks, and we might talk about this for a minute. "If the assassination was a state crime, why was the autopsy done by"—and I don't know if your wording here is correct—"by a non-pathologist in Washington, D.C. Why wasn't there an autopsy here?" That's a very interesting story and there are several of you that can, can get into that. Who wants to take it on?"

It was really Dr. Rose, was it, who was the county medical examiner here? Was that it, Charles Rose? Earl Rose, right. And he tried to do an autopsy here, and the president's entourage said we're getting him out of here, and they moved very quickly and did not permit the autopsy to be performed. I was looking the other day at the arrest record, and I should have brought it up. Thought I had it in my briefcase, and I've lost my briefcase, so, that takes care of that. You know there's a mistake on the arrest, on the police report of Kennedy's death? The Dallas PD report? It has his wrong age on there. Did you know that? Typographical error. He was 46 when he died and it said 47. Well, I guess that we ought to wrap this up. You've been a most delightful group, and all of us have enjoyed being with you, and now Darwin has a couple of closing remarks. Thank you very much.

Payne: Well, we've been waiting for the results of that poll. [A reference to the questionnaire distributed among participants concerning the assassination.] I've been anxiously walking to the back of the room, and we don't have it yet. Maybe you'll read about it in the paper if you don't hear about it here, but Gary Shultz has the information and was compiling it, and we'll have it later. After you've gone. There is much more to say, of course. but this has been a wonderful start, I think, and I deeply appreciate all the journalists who have come today. It has been a great event. Did I hear somebody call my name? No.

We've had a number of guests who were here, some of whom have been mentioned, but let me mention some others, and remind me if I miss any. Officer Jim Leavelle[21] is here. Officer Leavelle is the person, the homicide detective—you know who he was. You might stand, Jim. There he is at the back. Who, of course, was handcuffed to Oswald at the time he was shot. Bob Gemberling, who was the FBI agent who compiled the FBI report on Oswald. Where are you, Bob? Glad to have you. Tim Timmins, who was Assistant U.S. District Attorney. There's Tim. Greetings, Tim. We have heard from Sergeant Gerald Hill, who was here. Bobbie Hicks, who processed that film. Warren G. Harding, county treasurer and state treasurer. Did I miss anyone? I'm sure I've missed.

---

[21]The Dallas police officer who was escorting Oswald and was handcuffed to him as a security measure when Ruby shot him in the police basement.

Everyone who is here is special. And we—Gemberling, we introduced him, yeah. Now, I've got a letter, a note from an anonymous person. I'd like to read it. I think in tribute to all you journalists who came today. "You chose a career to cover the news. This fateful day in November has now made you historians. For those of us born in the 60's and 70's you have made a tragic day in history become real. Your presence here has rekindled old friendships and brought back old stories, but also you have captured and put into words the scene of the events that surrounded those history-making days. Thank you for taking the time to pass on history." I thought that was an awfully nice note. Now, this has been a very exciting weekend for us, an enjoyable one, but we cannot forget that it was a tragedy that was the genesis for this weekend. And also we remember that many of our good friends, our journalist friends who covered this story with us are no longer here. You've heard their names mentioned throughout the day. Could we ask you to pause and to reflect for just a few moments in memory of those journalists and also of our president? [silence] Thank you.

I'd like to mention a few other people, if you will indulge me. This whole thing began with a conversation between Jim Ewell and Alex Burton.[22] Alex hasn't come to the microphone today, a rare occasion for Alex, but, Alex, thank you. Stand up. We started meeting here at SMU to plan the event, and we composed a committee, a Reporters Remember committee, and it consisted of Jim and Alex, myself, Hugh Aynesworth, Eddie Barker, Bob Porter, Gary Shultz, [Bert Shipp] and Tony Zoppi. We appreciate all their work. Thanks also to our videotape crew, led by Lynn Smith and assisted by Wendy Adams. Thanks to Ralph Miller of SMU, Lynn Gartley of SMU's TV-radio sequence, John Gartley, director of Communication Arts. Thanks especially to Susan Todaro [and] Jeff Mohraz of SMU's catering service. And a very big thanks to the Dallas County Historical Foundation for a wonderful party which we had last night at the Sixth Floor. It was just terrific. It was an

---

22 A Dallas radio and television newsman who was on the Reporters Remember planning committee.

out-of-body experience to be up there, on the ground floor and then moving up to the sixth floor with all the journalists who had worked on this story. It was really a never-to-be-forgotten event. Thanks to WFAA-TV for a contribution to this program. Farris Ruckstool who brought us all the memorabilia you see out here in the cabinets, who also took the picture and you—again—you can order the picture from the Center for Communication Arts at SMU. We'll give you the details later. Thanks to Professor Hlavach and her SMU student volunteers, including the Society for Professional Journalists here at SMU. Peggy Montgomery and Barbara Scribner as well. Anything else? Any other comments? Closing?

The results. We have got the results. Partial. Well, these partial only from notes that were taken. Someone had better go check on Gary. I'm worried about his health. I don't know. This is from the audience. "Do you believe that Lee Harvey Oswald acted alone in assassinating President Kennedy?" Seventy-five yes, six no. And, that's about— "Do you believe Lee Harvey Oswald was involved in a conspiracy to assassinate the president?" Somehow these figures don't match. Nine yes, 72 no, so there's something wrong there. If you answered yes to No. 2, who was involved? Mafia. Gee, 32 Mafia, 14 Cuba, 42 U.S. intelligence agencies, 5 Dallas police. So I think we can disregard those numbers. They don't seem to reflect anything, to tell you the truth. [Their totals numbered more than the participants because of the wording of the questions which permitted multiple answers.] The information office was going to put a news release on the results of that poll, so I guess we can read about it there. That's all I have, and thanks again to all of you. It has been a wonderful day for us, and we appreciate your coming.

PARTICIPANTS

Phil Allen, night news editor, KBOX Radio. Worked from studio Friday, went to police station Saturday morning.

James W. "Ike" Altgens, photographer, Associated Press. Was 15 feet from JFK when shots were fired. First eyewitness to report shooting; only photographer with photos 24 hours after the assassination. (See pages 56-59.) (Deceased, December 12, 1995, age 76.)

Tom Alyea, cameraman, WFAA-TV. Filmed floor-by-floor search inside School Book Depository. Filmed evidence before it was touched by crime lab personnel, including the rifle hidden under boxes and the window barricade made of boxes. Filmed dying Oswald on stretcher. (See pages 36-41.)

Hugh Aynesworth, reporter, *Dallas Morning News*. Was near School Book Depository when shots were fired. Interviewed witnesses. Saw Oswald's capture in Texas Theater. Was in police basement when Oswald was shot. Covered Ruby trial, Clay Shaw trial. (See pages 28-31, 76-78, and 128-30.)

Eddie Barker, news director, KRLD-TV and Radio. Responsible for assignments, preparations, etc., of JFK visit. Was at Trade Mart, went on air as motorcade sped by on way to Parkland. Credited with first announcement of JFK death on CBS. Did first TV interview with Marina. (See pages 5-9.)

Kent Biffle, reporter, *Dallas Morning News*. Rode in motorcade from Love Field, was allowed into School Book Depository immediately after shots were fired and followed progress of investigation there. Later covered Ruby trial as well as Clay Shaw trial in New Orleans. (See pages 50-52.)

Warren Bosworth, reporter, *Dallas Times Herald.* Out of city on day of assassination. Returned and covered Oswald's murder on Sunday. Later wrote first story linking Oswald with attempted murder of Edwin A. Walker.

Anita Brewer, reporter, *Austin American-Statesman.* Flew to Dallas with fellow staffer Sam Wood on Friday afternoon after shots were fired. Called U.S. District Judge Sarah T. Hughes at her home and went there for interview.

Alex Burton, film-cutter and scriptwriter for the Texas News nightly news on WBAP-TV. Went to work that Friday afternoon at 2 p.m. and worked in office. Stayed until past midnight that night. Was told by news director at about 5 or 6 p.m. that he and others could go home since network would carry it all, but no one left.

Bo Byers, reporter, *Houston Chronicle.* On White House press bus when shots fired. Went to Parkland Hospital; rode with Senator Yarborough, Dallas Mayor Cabell, and others to Love Field for swearing-in of LBJ. Attended John Connally press conference at Parkland on Sunday morning. Was at Parkland's emergency entrance when Oswald was brought in on stretcher after being shot by Jack Ruby. (See pages 33-36, 134.)

Jerry Cabluck, photographer, *Fort Worth Star-Telegram..* Covered JFK breakfast in Fort Worth. Went to Love Field, Parkland Hospital. Took aerial shots of key scenes.

Vivian Castleberry, women's editor, *Dallas Times Herald.* Was at Trade Mart, making notes on arrangements when press members arrived from the motorcade. Interviewed U.S. District Judge Sarah T. Hughes before she swore in LBJ, and interviewed her afterwards. (See pages 54-56.)

Mike Cochran, Associated Press. Was with Secret Service men Thursday night at The Cellar coffee house in Fort Worth. Attended JFK Friday breakfast in Fort Worth. Went to Parkland Hospital after shooting and covered Connally medical briefings. Was at Oswald funeral on Monday; served as pallbearer. (See pages 135, 137, 138, 142-43, 149-150).

Horace Craig, reporter, *Fort Worth Star-Telegram.* Heard news on radio of assassination, went to office and worked rewrite. Was weekend city editor when news came of Ruby shooting Oswald. Called in rest of reportorial staff and dispatched them to background Ruby. (See page 24-25.)

Charles F. Dameron, news editor, *Dallas Times Herald.* Had responsibility for planning overall coverage of JFK visit. Set deadlines, "shove-in" times, etc. Re-directed publishing schedule after news of shooting came. Worked over weekend in planning coverage and publication. (See pages 20-24, 26-27)

Jimmy G. Darnell, reporter/camerman, WBAP-TV. Rode in motorcade behind JFK. Heard shots, filmed chaos. Went to courthouse press room and filmed witnesses. Returned to Love Field; filmed JFK body being loaded aboard Air Force One. Dallas police confiscated his film, never to return it. Was at Parkland Hospital on Sunday when Oswald was brought in on a stretcher. (See pages 66-68.)

John De La Garza Jr., reporter, *The Daily Texan* (student newspaper, the University of Texas at Austin). Flew to Dallas upon learning of assassination. Located the priest, Oscar Huber, who administered last rites to President Kennedy. (See pages 158-59.)

Gary DeLaune, reporter, KLIF Radio. Was at police station Friday afternoon and evening for Oswald's arrival and midnight press conference. Jack Ruby, visiting KLIF studios and desperate for something to do, was sent to police station to give sandwich to DeLaune. On Sunday DeLaune was in police basement when Oswald was shot. (See pages 80-84.)

Tom C. Dillard, chief photographer, *Dallas Morning News.* Covered Kennedy arrival at Love Field, rode in motorcade six cars behind JFK. Took photo of sixth-floor window seconds after assassination. Took photos at Parkland on Friday afternoon. Took pictures of bullet marks on curb at Commerce Street. (See pages 17-20.)

Bill Evans, copyeditor, *Dallas Morning News.* Was at Love Field out of curiosity to see Kennedy arrival. Went to newspaper office when he learned of shots. Worked on pages for an "extra" which was never published for fear it would repeat too many rumors and be disruptive.

James (Jim) Ewell, police reporter, *Dallas Morning News.* Observed Kennedy arrival at Love Field. Minutes later saw presidential procession in disarray racing toward Parkland Hospital. Went to police station, then to School Book Depository. Was inside Texas Theater when Oswald was captured. (See pages 68-70, 79-80.)

Jim Featherston, courthouse reporter, *Dallas Times Herald.* Heard shots from his post at Main and Houston streets. Obtained Polaroid photo from Mary Moorman, gathered eyewitness accounts. Worked at courthouse on Saturday. Covered Ruby trial. (See pages 48-49.)

Gene Gordon, chief photographer, *Fort Worth Press.* Covered JFK arrival in Fort Worth and the breakfast on Friday morning. Took photos at Parkland Hospital on Friday afternoon. Covered Oswald funeral.

Clint Grant, photographer, *Dallas Morning News.* Was with presidential party from Washington, D.C. Took photo at Love Field showing JFK, LBJ, Connally, their wives, Erik Jonsson, Police Chief Jesse Curry. Traveled in motorcade in open convertible with three White House photographers. Heard three shots. Took photos at Parkland Hospital. Saw LBJ come out of hospital en route to airplane. Saw Judge Sarah T. Hughes as she came off Air Force One after swearing in the new president. (See pages 31-33.)

R.E. (Buster) Haas, desk editor, *Dallas Morning News.* Witnessed parade from Dealey Plaza with wife and son. Was told to get every story and picture in the paper, regardless of how many pages it took. Worked many, many hours without much sleep over weekend. (See pages 15-16.) (Deceased, March 24, 1996, at age 70, apparent heart attack.)

Jerry Haynes, announcer, on-air personality, WFAA-TV. Was standing at corner of Main and Houston when he heard shots fired. Ran back to nearby station to alert newsroom. Interviewed some of the very first eyewitnesses in live broadcasts from WFAA-TV.

Bill Hendricks, reporter, *Fort Worth Press.* Wrote profile of Oswald for special edition published early Saturday. Flew to Cleveland with Dallas Cowboys for Sunday football game and had eerie experience there. Covered Oswald funeral in Fort Worth on Monday.

Robert S. Huffaker, newsman, KRLD TV and Radio. Broadcast live radio report of motorcade from Main and Akard streets, then went to Parkland and broadcast from there, interviewing Congressman Jim Wright, Senator Ralph Yarborough, and others. Went to police headquarters. On CBS radio and TV got Chief Curry to assert that FBI knew of Oswald and his whereabouts. Broadcast shooting of Oswald from basement on Sunday. (See pages 63-66.)

Eddie S. Hughes, reporter, *Dallas Morning News.* Was on city desk at time of shooting. Handled mobile call from fellow reporter Robert E. Baskin, who was two cars back and thought he heard shots from front and back. Covered Oswald funeral; served as pallbearer. (See page 142.)

Bob Jackson, photographer, *Dallas Times Herald.* Saw rifle from sixth floor window of Texas School Book Depository as he rode in photographers' car in presidential motorcade. Was at police station Sunday and took historic photo of Ruby shooting Oswald. (See pages 111-113.)

Robert A. Jarboe, photographer, Associated Press. Photographed horrified spectators at Dealey Plaza thirty minutes after shooting. Processed and printed film of LBJ swearing-in on Air Force One for pool distribution. Was at Oswald press conference Friday night, and saw Jack Ruby offering to help with food, drinks, or interviews. Printed and transmitted *Dallas Morning News* photographer Jack Beer's photo of Ruby advancing on Oswald.

Ron McAllister Jenkins, reporter, KBOX Radio. Reported landing of Air Force One at Love Field, then "spot-reported" along motorcade. Went to Parkland Hospital, reported from there. Spent Friday evening at Dallas police station. Was in Parkland Hospital when body of Officer Tippit arrived. On Sunday was in phone booth in basement of police station when Ruby shot Oswald. (See pages 70-72.)

Ferd Kaufman, photographer, Associated Press. Was in Fort Worth for breakfast; then at Trade Mart. Saw police leaving Texas Theater with Oswald. Beat them to police station and got photo of Oswald as he arrived. (See pages 89-90.)

Karl King, UPI Audio. Was on air with KBOX at 12:30 p.m. Friday when shots were fired. Sam Pate in audio unit told him of shots and he immediately broadcast this news, even before Merriman Smith's flash on UPI newswire.

Travis Linn, reporter, WFAA Radio. Did pool radio broadcasts for six local stations and ABC from Trade Mart. Went to Love Field and saw departure of Air Force One. Was in Oswald's room in afternoon. Friday evening and Saturday covered police station.

Charmayne Marsh, news editor, *Daily Texan* (University of Texas at Austin student newspaper). Chartered airplane to fly to Dallas Friday afternoon with two other student journalists. Hitched a ride to School Book Depository. Went to sixth floor. Saw Oswald at police station and also Marguerite Oswald.

Jon (Bunky) McConal, reporter, *Fort Worth Star-Telegram*. Served as pallbearer for Oswald funeral, and at the request of the funeral director solicited other newsmen to help with the casket. (See pages 143-44.)

Preston McGraw, United Press International. Joined JFK press corps in Fort Worth on Thursday evening. Covered breakfast in Fort Worth; wrote a "hold for release" piece on JFK's never-delivered speech at Trade Mart. Was at Trade Mart when shots were fired. Went to Parkland to get official announcement of JFK death. On Saturday interviewed Ruth Paine, whose house Marina Oswald had been living in. Covered Oswald funeral on Monday, and served as pallbearer. (See pages 14-15.)

Jerry McNeill, photographer, United Press International Newspictures. Covered JFK in Fort Worth, then went to Trade Mart to await his arrival. Upon learning of shooting went to Parkland Hospital. Was at Oswald burial in Fort Worth.

Tom Milligan, farm editor, *Dallas Morning News*. Was at Trade Mart for luncheon. Raced to Parkland Hospital on news of shooting. Sat with Mrs. Earle Cabell at back of hospital until press conference was over. Returning to the *News*, he manned telephones for hour or so. At 7 p.m. was assigned to assist out-of-town reporters. Took phone calls from all over world. Appalled by behavior and outright theft of materials by visiting reporters. (See pages 101-104, 136, 141, 150.)

Roy C. Nichols, reporter, KLIF Radio. Covered presidential arrival at Love Field. Went to Parkland on news of shooting, phoned in news that JFK was dead from mobile news unit. Was at church in choir when news came that Ruby shot Oswald. Left to cover the story.

Ike Pappas, radio reporter, WNEW in New York City. Flew to Dallas on Friday afternoon after hearing news of shooting of president. Went to police station, met Jack Ruby in unusual way, interviewed Henry Wade. Was present in basement of Dallas police station on Sunday when Ruby shot Oswald, and shouted question to Oswald immediately before shots rang out. (See pages 116-125.)

Darwin Payne, reporter, *Dallas Times Herald*. Went to School Book Depository Building after shots were fired. Located Abraham Zapruder; stayed at his office for couple of hours trying to get film and observing Dealey Plaza from his window. Went inside School Book Depository and to the sixth floor in mid-afternoon. At Oswald's rooming house Friday night. Wrote profile on Oswald for Saturday paper. Was at police station Saturday from about 5 p.m. to 2 a.m. Went to Ruby's apartment on Sunday after he shot Oswald. Interviewed neighbors there. (See pages 1-4, 91-94.)

George Phenix, cameraman, KRLD-TV. Filmed Kennedy's arrival at Love Field. Hitched ride to Parkland with Air Force general from Trade Mart. Filmed events outside Parkland from second-story window with good vantage point. Was in police basement when Ruby shot Oswald.

Mary Woodward Pillsworth, reporter, *Dallas Morning News*. Was at Dealey Plaza in group of four women's staffers who probably were closest to the President of any spectators when shots were fired. Saw impact of shots. Wrote eyewitness report for next day's newspaper. (See pages 41-44.)

Bob Porter, amusements writer, *Dallas Times Herald*. Was in newspaper office at time of assassination. Knew Ruby, talked with him Friday afternoon concerning his decision on whether or not to close his nightclub for that weekend. (See pages 125-27.)

Ted W. Powers, reporter, Associated Press. Covered JFK in San Antonio, then went to former Vice President John Nance Garner's home in Uvalde. Was there when JFK called him on Nov. 22. Went to Dallas upon news of assassination.

Mike Quinn, reporter, *Dallas Morning News*. Was at Love Field for JFK arrival, traveled in motorcade. Went to Parkland and interviewed Sen. Yarborough and others. Went into hospital press room and took up coverage of Connally. Took off next morning for Washington, D.C.

Lawrence J. Schiller, writer, *Saturday Evening Post*. As photojournalist flew to Dallas on Friday upon news of assassination. Covered all events in Dallas for 10 days. Work appeared in *SatEvePost* and also was syndicated. Was at police station, School Book Depository, Oswald's room, and Ruby's apartment.

John Schoellkopf, reporter, *Dallas Times Herald*. Arrived at the Texas Theater on Friday afternoon in time to see a bleeding Oswald led away by police. On Sunday morning, as only working editor at *Times Herald*, told photographer Bob Jackson to leave city police station to go to Nellie Connally press conference at Parkland Hospital. Jackson delayed his departure in time to take his historic photo of Ruby shooting Oswald. When Jackson arrived at office Schoellkopf said he was "practically in tears" because he believed someone had jumped in front of him to obscure the picture.

Keith Shelton, political writer, *Dallas Times Herald*. Traveled with JFK presidential party in San Antonio, Houston, Fort Worth, and into Dallas. Wrote story based on advance text for his Trade Mart speech. Covered events at Trade Mart. Did various aftermath stories, covered opening of Ruby trial.

Roger J. (Joe) Sherman, reporter, *Dallas Times Herald*. Was at Trade Mart to cover JFK arrival. Upon learning of trouble called office, was sent to Schoolbook Depository. Went to sixth floor that afternoon. Covered FBI angles on Saturday. (Deceased, August 5, 1996, age 61, heart attack.)

Bert N. Shipp, assistant news director, WFAA-TV. Made assignments pertinent to coverage of presidential visit. Was at Trade Mart when word came of shooting. Saw limousines speed by en route to Parkland Hospital. Went to Parkland, filmed events there. Tried to take phone from Merriman Smith. Sheriff Bill Decker told him JFK was dead before official announcement was made. Relayed this word to WFAA and told newsman to go on air with it. Newsman would not, so Shipp did it himself at 1:09 p.m. Friday. (See pages 60-63.)

Tom J. Simmons, assistant managing editor, *Dallas Morning News.* Was at Trade Mart for luncheon. Saw agitation as newsmen arrived, heard on police motorcycle that JFK had been shot. Was first in room to learn the news. Went to *News* office and directed coverage in absence of Managing Editor Jack Krueger, who was on federal jury duty. (See pages 9-12.)

S. Griffin (Griff) Singer, assistant city editor, *Dallas Morning News.* Helped keep track of 25-plus city-side reporters scattered all over Dallas, a difficult chore. Was especially impressed at how well local reporters-editors responded to the challenge.

Bill Sloan, copyeditor, *Dallas Times Herald.* Wrote headline for JFK's arrival, which said approximately, "Cheering Throngs Welcome Kennedy to Dallas." Saw motorcade pass from newsroom window. Saw pandemonium in office upon news of shots. Helped edit lead story written by editor Felix McKnight with notes dictated by police reporter George Carter.

Richard H. Strobel, Associated Press. Flew to Dallas from Los Angeles with news of assassination. Reported to Dallas AP photo bureau, where scene was one of pandemonium. On Saturday morning negotiated with Zapruder for his film. Viewed film in Zapruder's office with others. Entered into bidding war with NBC and Time-Life.

David Taylor, photo editor, Southwest Division, Associated Press. Set up coverage for JFK visit to Texas. Traveled with JFK in Houston. Worked in AP office transmitting photos on Friday afternoon. Was there when White House photographers came in with film of LBJ being sworn in on Air Force One. Screened the Zapruder movie film and helped AP make unsucessful bid to buy it.(See pages 16-17.)

Ed L. Teer, reporter, KRLD-TV and Radio. Happened to be downtown, not on duty, watching motorcade from Adolphus Hotel. Was assigned by Eddie Barker to field in-coming calls from all over world. Broke news to CBS listeners in Canada of president's death. Went to Parkland and Love Field to cover arrival of Connally children as they flew in. Told them that their mother was alive and that their father likely would live.

Russ Thornton, producer, WBAP-TV. As producer of 10 o'clock Texas News was ready to go to work when news of shots came. First task was to get additional help for Dallas staff and to satisfy needs of NBC. (See pages 12-14.)

Jack B. Tinsley, reporter, *Fort Worth Star-Telegram.* Covered Kennedy arrival at Hotel Texas on Thursday evening and breakfast next morning. Went to Parkland, saw casket wheeled down the hall. Hitchhiked downtown, went to School Book Depository, visited sixth floor, interviewed individuals. Found women in Zapruder's dress factory next door. Saw Oswald's midnight press conference. (See pages 85-88, 140.)

Harold T. Waters, photographer, Associated Press. Took arrival photos of JFK at Love Field. Was in AP office when fellow photographer James Altgens came in with first still photo of assassination. Processed and printed Altgen's film for transmission. Spent Friday night and Saturday at city hall.

Bob Welch, camerman/reporter, WBAP TV and Radio. At Love Field for JFK arrival. Followed presidential limousine to Parkland Hospital. Went live on radio with news of shooting. Arrived at Parkland just after presidential limousine. Recorded press conference announcing JFK's death. Went to city hall, stayed there over weekend. (See pages 52-54.)

John Weeks, editorial page staff member, *Dallas Times Herald.* After shots were fired was mobilized to edit story containing reaction from Trade Mart. Revised editorial pages for weekend, working all night and going home at 5 a.m. Saturday. Realized editorial page had printed a letter some time earlier from an "O.H. Lee" who urged "fair play" for Cuba. Tried to find original, but couldn't. (See pages 159-160.)

Michael Whittaker, United Press International. Watched parade, was one of first inside School Book Depository. Saw LBJ at Parkland talking to Chief Curry about getting to airport. Attended (in pajama tops) news conference on Sunday in which Oswald's death was announced. Attended Tippit's funeral. (Day of assassination was his third day on job.)

Bill Winfrey, photographer, *Dallas Morning News.* Was at Trade Mart to cover JFK speech. Went to Parkland and made pictures of presidential limousine with pool of blood in back seat and pink roses lying in blood. Photos of Jackie with blood on her dress, of hundreds of people kneeling and praying by the emergency entrance. As Oswald arrived at police station took pictures of him with handcuffs in front of face. Stayed at police station all night Friday. Talked with Jack Ruby there. (See pages 45-47, 99-101.)

Wes Wise, camerman/reporter, KRLD-TV, Radio. Was at Trade Mart, where he had been asked by Secret Service and FBI to identify suspicious persons from earlier attacks on Adlai Stevenson in Dallas. Interviewed Police Sgt. Jerry Hill concerning the capture of Oswald at Texas Theater. Talked to Jack Ruby on Saturday at the School Book Depository. Assigned to Dallas County jail to await Oswald's arrival on Sunday. Was witness in Ruby trial. (See pages 97-98, 114-16.)

Tony Zoppi, columnist, *Dallas Morning News.* Watched motorcade from Adolphus Hotel marquee. Went to Parkland Hospital, helped carry president to trauma room. Alerted *News* to his death. Was at *News* when word of Oswald's shooting came over wire. Went to city hall, was interviewed by press concerning his friend Jack Ruby, who called him from his jail cell two or three days after shooting Oswald and told him why he did it. Ruby was regular visitor to Zoppi's office, seeking plugs for Carousel Club. (See pages 73-76, 106-111.)